GOLD CREEKS AND GHOST TOWNS OF Northeastern Washington

Covering: OKANOGAN, FERRY, STEVENS, PEND OREILLE, CHELAN AND KITTITAS COUNTIES

N.L. BARLEE

ISBN 0-88839-452-7

Cataloging in Publication Data
Barlee, N. L. (Neville Langrell), 1932–
Gold creeks and ghost towns of northeastern Washington

ISBN 0-88839-452-7

1. Mines and mineral resources--Washington (State)--History. 2. Gold mines and mining--Washington (State)--History. 3. Washington (State)--History. 4. Extinct cities--Washington (State) I. Title.
F891.B37 1999 979.7'2 C99-9101152-8

Printed in Hong Kong—ColorCraft

Published simultaneously in Canada and the United States by

HANCOCK HOUSE PUBLISHERS LTD.
19313 Zero Avenue, Surrey, B.C. V4P 1M7
(604) 538-1114 Fax (604) 538-2262

HANCOCK HOUSE PUBLISHERS
1431 Harrison Avenue, Blaine, WA 98230-5005
(604) 538-1114 Fax (604) 538-2262
Web Site: www.hancockhouse.com *email:* sales@hancockhouse.com

CONTENTS

FOREWORD

This work presents a brief look at the six historic mining counties of northeastern Washington; Kittitas, Chelan, Okanogan, Ferry, Stevens and Pend Oreille. Included within these counties are some of the most fascinating and historic areas on the old Pacific Slope.

During the several years of research and wandering through this region, I once again familiarized myself with places I had known as a boy, forty years ago. Northport, Nighthawk, Republic, Orient and many of those storied towns of the past were much the same as they had been, although fire and the elements had taken their toll.

So I travelled with the wind, drifting here and there, into many forgotten corners of this ever changing and enchanting old region. I was on Mary Ann, Swauk, Baker, Williams, Big Goosmus, Sheep, the Columbia, Shaser, Peshastin, the Similkameen, Salmon, Fortune, Boulder, the Kettle and a myriad of other golden creeks and rivers which had once resounded to the sound of mining when the West was being opened up.

I listened carefully to the innumerable stories of long lost mines and missing treasure trove. Afterwards I perused the many details before finally selecting a handful which met the strict criteria of names, dates, geology, plausibility and accuracy of minutiae, and occasionally, first hand witnesses.

In passing, I took in the atmosphere of long deserted ghost towns and mining towns like Bodie, Molson, Addy, Curlew, Chesaw, Bossburg, Chewelah, Danville, Conconully, Keller, Loomis, Ruby, Winthrop, Roslyn, Old Blewett and half a dozen others that fall into that unique category.

And along the way I found other old ghost towns and mining camps which are virtually unknown in the annals of ghost towns of Washington; unfrequented places like Leadpoint, Cedarville, Golden, Ferry, Boundary and Gilbert and I managed to locate some previously unpublished photographs of most of those shadowy old camps. These photographs are included in the body of this work.

I have not, however, included certain prominent towns and cities within the six counties which do have a mining history, places such as Wenatchee, Oroville, Colville and several others because they do not fit the status of mining towns, that is the towns which were established primarily because of a mining boom or stampede.

Finally, to those who have that unusual affinity and feel for ghost town history and the high country of this part of the state, I hope that the pages of this book will prove rewarding.

N. L. Barlee

I
OKANOGAN COUNTY

INTRODUCTION

Okanogan County - This is the land of Kamiakin and Tonasket; famous Indian chiefs from another century, and those men of the early west like "Okanogan" Smith and "Pinnacle Jim" O'Connell. It is the largest and one of the most fascinating counties in the state.

Here the footloose and curious may wander past long forgotten towns and abandoned townsites with colorful names like Ruby, Golden and Bodie or range through the sweeping desert lands or up into the remote high country.

There is much to hold the passerby; legends of hidden gold and long lost mines, several of them still searched for by close-mouthed treasure hunters and others intrigued by the age old quest for gold. And some of those historic towns of yesterday, places like Wauconda, Nighthawk and old Molson, still stand, silent monuments to the past and little changed in almost a hundred years.

Walk through the brooding recesses of McLaughlin's Canyon and along the banks of rivers with lyrical Indian names like Okanogan or Similkameen, and you still stalk the West of the 19th century - and that is Okanogan County.

The "rock" near Rich Bar on the Similkameen river. In this area were some of the richest placers in Washington Territory. Later, a number of lode gold and silver mines were discovered nearby.

GHOST TOWNS

Main Street in Loomis, Washington - circa 1908. These were the days when the mines close to Loomis, with names like Copper World, Second Prize, Palmer Mountain, Pinnacle and half a dozen other properties were spewing out a golden tithe and the town was booming. Today, old Loomis and its once busy Main Street no longer serve the miners who stampeded into the county before the turn of the century. (Okanogan County Museum photo)

and MINING TOWNS

BODIE

Straddling the road between Old Toroda and Corkscrew Mountain, is an old mining camp called Bodie. Half a dozen buildings still stand in this once celebrated camp, a testimonial to the longevity of the Bodie Mine. The history of this town, like so many of the early mining camps of the Pacific Slope, is the old story of boom and bust.

In 1888, eight years before the north half of the Colville Indian Reservation was throw open for mineral entry, a prospector named Henry DeWitz, attracted by the mineralized outcrops in the region, moved in with the Indians and soon established a log building settlement at the mouth of Bodie Creek. By 1896, "Bodie" was firmly established with the usual restaurant, general store, smithy shop, livery barn and several log cabins. From this headquarters the prospectors fanned out to scout the mountains nearby. But it was Henry DeWitz who struck the big lode, and barely a mile north of Bodie. He came across a quartz vein bearing free gold and in short order he staked a number of claims, in fact too many, so he sold one of them to his brother Ben for $50, to keep it in the family. Ben DeWitz dutifully began doing some development work and struck a pocket of ore which purportedly yielded an amazing $80,000 in

The deserted camp of Bodie today. Half a dozen buildings still stand close by the road, slowly decaying. Close by are the abandoned remains of the old Bodie Mine, once the mainstay of the camp. To the south lies Old Toroda, to the north, baffling Corkscrew Mountain.

Old Toroda stands abandoned - circa 1910

Log stores standing on the deserted main street of Old Toroda in 1939
(Both photographs courtesy - The Okanogan County Historical Society)

gold. On the strength of this windfall the DeWitz brothers sold the mine to another set of brothers; of chewing gum renown, the Wrigley Brothers of Chicago. Not lacking in capital, the Wrigleys built a reduction mill in 1902 and the mine began to make a name for itself. The mine, called the Bodie; a favorite name of Henry DeWitz, quickly became the center of mining activity in the Toroda Creek valley. Sensing the shift, the inhabitants of the original settlement of Bodie simply picked up and moved north to the minesite. Thus the second town of "Bodie" came into being.

By 1917, however, the pockety nature of the ore and a slow decline in values forced the mine to close. For seventeen more years old Bodie lay abandoned until an increase in the price of gold triggered activity in the region again and suddenly the Bodie Mine looked attractive once more. New owners took over and soon the sounds of mining echoed through the valley as the old Bodie Mine started production.

For another decade the Bodie Mine yielded tens of thousands of tons of ore averaging nearly half an ounce of gold per ton. But finally, in 1944, after producing an estimated $1,250,000.00 in gold, the mine shut down once more.

Since then the mill has fallen into decay but the camp, completely abandoned, still stands as a classic ghost camp - a silent tribute to those years when some brothers named DeWitz and Wrigley put their faith in a mine named the Bodie.

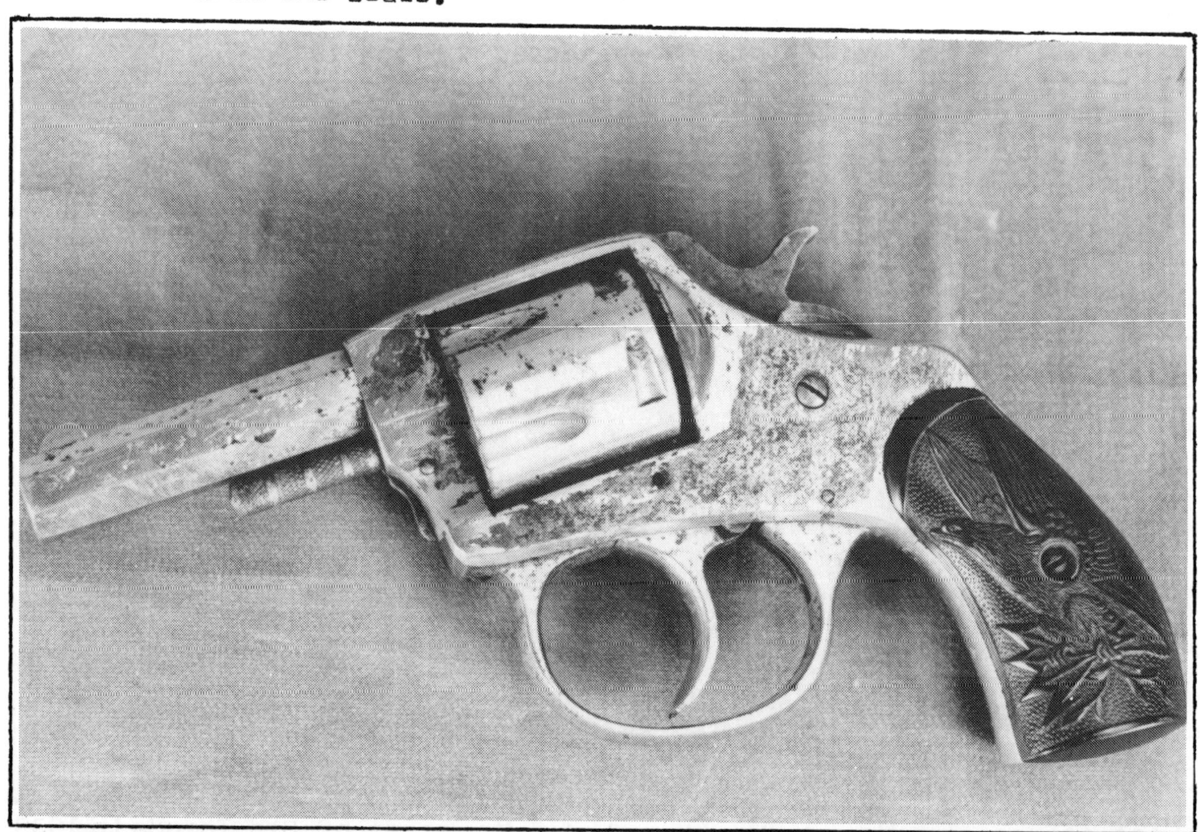

A "Two Dollar Special." This revolver was found in a miner's cabin in 1972 and was typical of the older type revolvers dug up or found.

BOLSTER

The BOLSTER DRILL is no more and Bolster itself has disappeared. Once in the early part of this century, the town challenged Chesaw for leadership in the Okanogan Highlands. In 1900 the masthead of the DRILL boldly stated that Bolster was "The metropolis of the Myers Creek Mining District." Indeed, in that year Bolster was a real comer. It boasted a total of between thirty and forty buildings and a boom was on. With nearly a dozen businesses strung out along its one main street it was humming.

Like Chesaw, the mines and prospects nearby, especially those on Buckhorn Mountain, several miles to the east, promised prosperity and longevity for the camp. J. C. Robinson's Assay Office assayed samples of gold and silver ore for $1.50, Hamilton and Nickle's General Store was doing a landslide business and the other merchants weren't too far behind.

But Bolster's fortunes were tied to the mines and when they failed at depth Bolster was finished. Later that year the boom had bust. And when notices offering the Hotel Bolster "For Sale Cheap For Cash" began to appear in the DRILL, Bolster was on the way down. By 1915 the town stood deserted; another in a long list of abandoned mining camps.

There's not much left now, but Bolster was there - once.

Not much remains of Bolster today. But those arid brown hills in the background were once alive with prospectors. You'd never guess that a town of three hundred stood here once.

An old store in Loomis, Okanogan County

An early building near Chesaw, Okanogan County

CHESAW

In an almost forgotten corner of the Okanogan Highlands stands historic Chesaw. A walk down its dusty main street still conjures up memories of those days when this town was on the edge of greatness in the mining world.

The name of the town is unusual but then so is its history. When placer gold was discovered in quantity in nearby Mary Ann creek before the turn of the century, the result was a headlong rush of placer men into the district. Much to their surprise and dismay they found that there were already numbers of Oriental miners in the area; the Chinese had been quietly mining the creeks for years. One of the most prominent of the Orientals was a certain Chee Saw, a former placer miner who had married an Indian woman and had a small ranch and store on a flat not too far from the diggings. The white miners soon began purchasing all their supplies from the amiable and clever Chinese merchant. Soon the phrase "Chee Saw's" became a byword for fair prices and square deals, and eventually it evolved into simply "Chesaw," the name the community bears to this day.

Although Mary Ann and several other placer creeks in the district yielded several thousand ounces of the yellow metal some of the placer

Freight wagons moving along main street in Chesaw in 1899. Chesaw was on the rise then. (Photograph - Okanogan County Historical Society)

The false-fronted Townsite Building on Chesaw's main street today. The surrounding area is one of the most fascinating regions in the state.

Early autumn falls on an abandoned house on the outskirts of Chesaw.

men, finding highly mineralized veins, began turning their attention to lode prospects. By the turn of the century the region had become a a lodestone for hardrock miners as magnificent discoveries were made. And "Chesaw" was the main beneficiary. Strategically located at the center of the mining activity, it quickly burgeoned into a bona fide mining town. When Major James Blaine, a former U. S. Army officer who had fought in the Apache Wars, moved in and established the first assay office in north central Washington and his equally ambitious daughter Georgia founded the MYERS CREEK NEWS, Chesaw was on its way. By 1910, there were forty buildings in Chesaw, many of them quite substantial. In those times the area was alive with prospectors and it seemed that strikes were being made on every hill in all directions. To the west, mines like the Poland-China, indicated great promise. To the east, on the beyond the headwaters of Bolster creek and on the flanks of Buckhorn Mountain, half a dozen mines with names like the Grant, Rainbow, Nip and Tuck, Crystal Butte, Monterey and Number Nine, based on their impressive assay results, were expected to contribute more than their share of wealth. To the north, between Chesaw and a rival mining camp called Bolster; other acclaimed properties like the Reco, Reserve and a handful of other gold mines simply added to the already impressive total.

The original workings of the Crystal Butte mine near Chesaw in 1899.
(Photograph - Courtesy Okanogan County Historical Society)

Several abandoned mine buildings on the old Poland-China property west of Chesaw.

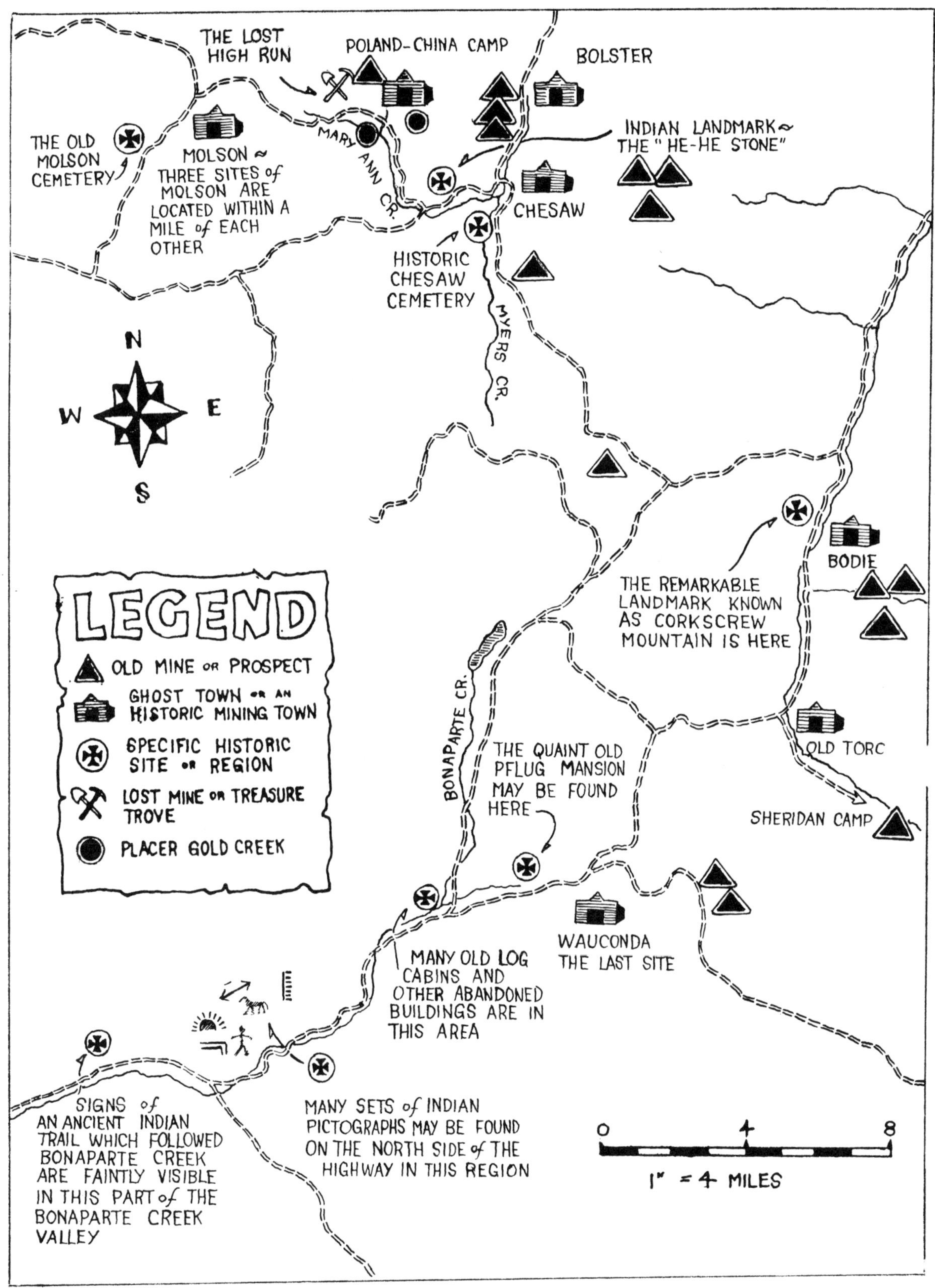

THE LOST HIGH RUN
POLAND-CHINA CAMP
BOLSTER
THE OLD MOLSON CEMETERY
MOLSON ~ THREE SITES of MOLSON ARE LOCATED WITHIN A MILE of EACH OTHER
MARY ANN CR.
INDIAN LANDMARK ~ THE "HE-HE STONE"
CHESAW
HISTORIC CHESAW CEMETERY
MYERS CR.
N
W
E
S
LEGEND
OLD MINE OR PROSPECT
GHOST TOWN OR AN HISTORIC MINING TOWN
SPECIFIC HISTORIC SITE OR REGION
LOST MINE OR TREASURE TROVE
PLACER GOLD CREEK
BODIE
THE REMARKABLE LANDMARK KNOWN AS CORKSCREW MOUNTAIN IS HERE
BONAPARTE CR.
OLD TORC
THE QUAINT OLD PFLUG MANSION MAY BE FOUND HERE
SHERIDAN CAMP
WAUCONDA THE LAST SITE
MANY OLD LOG CABINS AND OTHER ABANDONED BUILDINGS ARE IN THIS AREA
SIGNS of AN ANCIENT INDIAN TRAIL WHICH FOLLOWED BONAPARTE CREEK ARE FAINTLY VISIBLE IN THIS PART of THE BONAPARTE CREEK VALLEY
MANY SETS of INDIAN PICTOGRAPHS MAY BE FOUND ON THE NORTH SIDE of THE HIGHWAY IN THIS REGION
0
4
8
1" = 4 MILES

The picturesque Chesaw cemetery south of the old mining town.

The assay office which stands on the outskirts of Chesaw, close to the road to old Bolster.

Those were the days when Chesaw was on the rise and the sounds peculiar to a mining boom town could be heard; the curses and shouts of bearded teamsters urging their teams on as they pulled heavily laden freight wagons through town on their way to distant mines; the steady buzz of conversation and the click of poker chips in the saloons where a mine was bought or sold on a handshake deal or a stack of gold coins changed hands on the turn of a card, and above all, the noises of the town building as new structures appeared almost daily. Clearly Chesaw was destined to become the great town of the Okanogan Highlands.

But those years, alas, were short-lived. The mines, the economic mainstay of the town, with assays so encouraging on the upper levels, simply didn't carry their values to depth despite the persistent and heroic efforts of their owners. And one by one, most of the mines were abandoned and Chesaw began to slip. When the CHESAW NEWS finally threw in the towel it was fairly obvious, even to the diehards, that Chesaw had passed its peak.

So Chesaw, like so many hard luck mining towns, declined. As the years passed, the buildings lining main street, savaged by fire and the elements, slowly disappeared. But this is an area where time seems to have paused; the moody Poland-China Camp still stands just north of Mary Ann creek, Chesaw's picturesque cemetery lies virtually unchanged and that entire region, studded with abandoned ranches, deserted mines and placer workings, is reminiscent of those days when gold was king in the Okanogan Highlands.

Customs officer - circa 1890s. His badge may be seen on his left lapel.

CONCONULLY

At first glance you'd probably never guess that this little town, hidden in the hills of the western Okanogan, was once the county seat. There is much about Conconully that never meets the eye. It was a boom town once. During the 1890s the phrase "Okanogan County" conjured up visions of hidden wealth and it was a beacon for prospectors all over the west. They came streaming in, first to Ruby, an overnight mining camp just south of Conconully.

It came into being as "Salmon City" after mineralized ledges of high grade ore were discovered in the Salmon River area, especially on Mineral Hill and Homestake Mountain. These discoveries, made in 1886, resulted in the formation of the Salmon River Mining District. Before long Salmon City was born. With properties and mines like the Salmon River Group, the John Arthur mine, the Lone Star mine, the Tough Nut mine, the Homestake mine and increasing numbers of other mines coming into production, Salmon City looked enviously at Ruby City, the county seat. Certainly Salmon City was more suited to be the county seat than its smaller rival and its ambitious citizens began working toward that goal.

By 1891, the name of the camp had been changed to "Conconully,"

Conconully at its apex; when the mines nearby were going full blast.
(photograph - Courtesy Okanogan County Historical Society)

Well known photographs of Conconully by the talented Frank Matsura. Matsura, a Japanese photographer who settled in Okanogan County was the photographic chronicler of the county. The finest collection of his photographs are found in the county museum in Okanogan, Wash.
(photographs - Courtesy Okanogan County Historical Society)

and it had become the County seat, replacing dwindling Ruby. The 1890s were interesting years for Conconully. The shootout between a bandit named Herb LeRoy and Sheriff Fred Thorp caused barely a ripple in that tough camp but when an Indian was lynched for a suspected murder on a cold January day, it made headlines. It was one tough town.

For several years Conconully prospered. The silver was flowing in steadily and main street became quite a showplace. Even the financial panic of 1893 and the subsequent drop in the price of silver failed to halt its progress, but when a wall of water and debris swept down the main street in the spring of 1894, destroying many of the businesses in its path, the town was never quite the same thereafter.

The OKANOGAN RECORD kept publishing but the news wasn't quite as upbeat as it had been; the stagecoaches continued to make their trips to places like Oroville and Brewster, but not quite as often as they had a few years before. And the mines began to suffer from the malady of the Okanogan, "poor values at depth." It was a harbinger.

So, gradually, Conconully began to fade. When the county seat was lost to the town of Okanogan in 1914, a gloom settled over the town. The exodus increased after that and by the 1920s much of the splendor of the Conconully of old had vanished.

The town is still there today, nestled in those hills. Not much remains from the 1890s but the surrounding area, the site of old Ruby and the abandoned mines everywhere attest to the claim that Conconully was once "the most important town in the Okanogan."

An early view of Conconully at its apex; when it was still the county seat. By the 1920s, however, the town had lost much of its splendor.
(Photograph - Courtesy Okanogan County Historical Society)

GOLDEN

To the casual eye it would be difficult to imagine where the town had once stood. Oh yes, Golden was a bona fide mining town in its day, but that was in those halcyon years before the turn of the century.

And the story was typical. In 1887, tramp prospectors ranging the high country to the east of old Conconully, came across some outcrops of rotten oxidized quartz along a highly mineralized belt to the west of Wannacut Lake - and the quartz was laced with "free gold."

It was a magnificent find and word spread quickly. A rush turned, almost overnight, into a stampede as hundreds of prospectors streamed into the region. They located spectacular high grade ore at grassroots and within months mines with names like Triune, Spokane, Kimberly and half a dozen others were yielding steadily while to the north the Horn Silver and Maquae were adding to the total output.

On the strength of these showings a fledgling mining town sprang to life and by 1892 more than thirty buildings graced a flat between the mines and Wannacut Lake. The district held high promise then so it was only fitting that the camp was called "Golden."

The camp of Golden once stood on the flats beyond. Barely visible are the long abandoned mines against the hills. Gold and silver were the lure in this area almost a century ago.

At its height in those early days nearly three hundred inhabitants sauntered down its dusty main street where a general store, restaurant, saloon, post office and a number of other false-fronted businesses met the eye. With six mines within half a mile of town, Golden was a sure bet.

And for a brief time Golden prospered. Then, gradually and almost imperceptibly, it began to slip. At first it was barely noticeable but when ore values began to decline alarmingly at depth shipments from the mines dropped off sharply. It boded ill for the future because the mines were the economic mainstay of the town.

By 1910 under one hundred people remained and the downhill slide was irreversible. There were times after that when there were flurries of activity, especially during the 1930s, but they were generally short intervals and eventually Golden lay abandoned; another in a long list of mining ghost towns.

Today little remains at the old site, an outline where a building once stood but little else to mark the town. Those die-hard miners of yesteryear like old Dell Hart and A. M. Wehe prospect the barren hills and gulches no more, the stagecoaches no longer rattle into town from Ruby and Conconully and over all a silence prevails - the Golden of old has vanished.

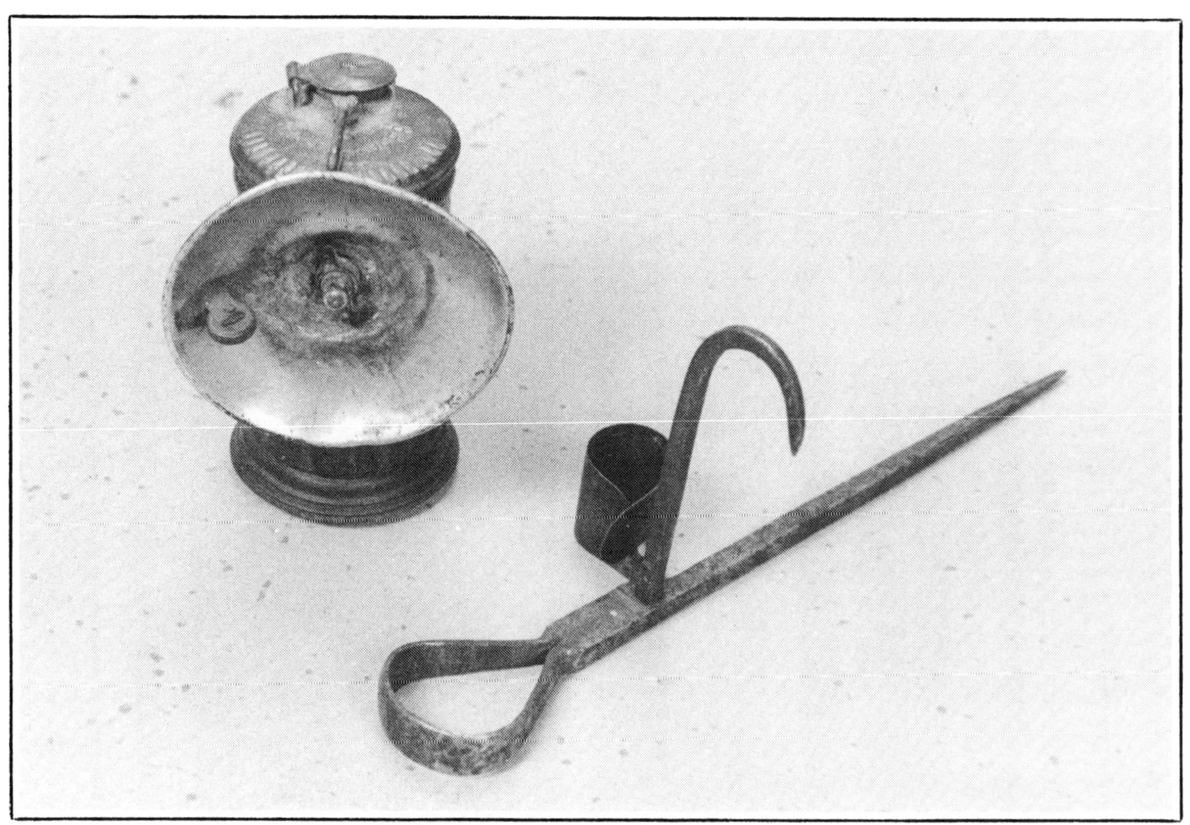

A carbide lamp and a "Sticking Johnny." Many artifacts like these have been found in the western part of Okanogan county. Golden, Nighthawk, Loomis, Ruby, Conconully and several other historic mining camps have all yielded innumerable mining artifacts over the past few decades.

LOOMIS

It was called "Loomiston" once. You could wander along its main street today and never guess that it was one of the great mining towns in Okanogan County at one time.

In the 1870s it was the winter cattle station for a huge cattle company called Phelps & Wadleigh. The valley to the north was suited to cattle and the cattlemen grazed their herds in the lush grasslands until the winter of 1879-80. That winter, however, was so severe that the herds were decimated and Phelps & Wadleigh, bankrupted, pulled out and never returned. But others drifted in, saw its possibilities, and stayed. One of these first settlers was Alvin Thorp, another was the pioneer merchant, J. A. Loomis, who built the first store on the site and called the place "Loomiston." He was soon joined Guy Waring, later of Winthrop fame, who became his partner. They stocked their store and settled down to wait. But they didn't have long to wait.

"Okanogan" Smith and others had known that the surrounding area was highly mineralized and were waiting for the reservation to open up to prospectors. In 1886 the reservation was thrown open and hundreds of prospectors flooded in. Some of these men, with names like "Tenas

The Ruby mine north of Loomis today. The entire region is dotted with abandoned mines, ore dumps and old mining roads.

George" Runnells and "Dutch Jake" Neiderauer, were veterans, miners who had followed the rainbow all of their lives. Many of the others were greenhorns, drawn by whispers of "free gold" in the western hills of the Okanogan.

By 1891 the influx had turned Loomis into a hive of activity. Its three block long main street was lined with buildings, including a total of eight saloons and two dancehalls. And in from the hills came news of discoveries on Palmer Mountain, Whiskey Hill, Mount Chopaka, Gold Hill and other areas close by as mines like the Jessie, Copper World, Black Bear, Pinnacle, War Eagle, Defiance, Empire and scores of other properties reported bonanza ore which was staggeringly high in silver and gold values: some owners simply used a mortar and pestle to crush the quartz and then poured crude bars of gold. That news circulated in weeks and before long capitalists from Spokane, Seattle and numerous other financial centers were pouring in to invest in the mines.

When it was reported that "Pard" Cummings, a stagecoach whip, had turned down a fare who admitted that he only had a hundred thousand or so to invest with the rejoinder; "You better walk - I'm only hauling millionaires and up!" It was not unusual for old Loomis in those days when the sky was the limit and everyone was a potential millionaire.

But in 1893 the bottom suddenly dropped out of the silver market

A few of the boys lounging around in front of Willard's Drugs in early day Loomis. In those years every man was a potential millionaire.
(photograph - Courtesy Okanogan County Historical Society)

and the ensuing financial panic threw Loomis into the doldrums. And it stayed that way until 1898, when interest in mining suddenly revived. After several new strikes were made on Palmer Mountain, Loomis roared back to life. By 1899 its population was over 500 and Palmer Mountain and the highly touted "Palmer Mountain Tunnel" were both forecast as the coming El Dorados of the far west. Loomis was a tough mining town then, typical of many little mining camps scattered through the state in those days, and it had more than its share of hardcases were more than willing to settle disputes with lead rather than lawyers. When a certain "Pinnacle Jim" O'Connell, the renowned locator of the Pinnacle mine, and another Irishman named John O'Herrin, stepped outside of the Woodard saloon, to settle a long standing feud it was not an unusual occurrence. O'Connell went for his trusty Bowie knife, O'Herrin wisely reached for his Colt. O'Connell realized too late that steel is seldom equal to lead in a fracus and after the smoke had cleared, O' Connell lay dead on the boardwalk, his body perforated by three bullets. John O'Herrin pleaded "not guilty" to homocide; citing self-defence, and a sympathetic jury quickly exonerated him. Another day in old Loomis.

But the mines around Loomis, like most of those gold and silver mines in the western part of Okanogan County didn't "go down," as the pioneer miners used to say. And they didn't in Loomis despite almost

Detail of the impressive business district of Loomis, probably around 1900.
(photograph - Courtesy Okanogan County Historical Society)

Yes, this was Loomis when its main street was crowded. There is little remaining from those years on main street, but outside, in every direction, history looms.

An open stagecoach - circa 1908, prepares to depart for Golden and other points.

(photographs - OCHS)

unbelievable assays, and the Palmer Mountain Tunnel, despite the high expectations, proved to be a bust. After that Loomis declined rapidly in both importance and population as the miners drifted away.

Today the Loomis of old has all but vanished. That colorful main street of the turn of the century is no more although a few buildings from that era still survive.

But the region in all directions is compelling. To the south lies historic Conconully and long gone Ruby. To the north, in that dry, arid desert, much history still remains. The abandoned mill at the Ruby mine stands yet in the shadows of Mount Chopaka although the settlement at Chopaka City is revealed only by faint outlines. But gaze across the valley to the east and the scars of the mines can still be seen along the barren slopes where those miners of yesterday toiled. And beyond Loomis itself wanderers may still find evidence of the mining era and the early days. Whiskey Hill hasn't moved and Gold Hill is almost the same as it was when the valley echoed with activity.

True, the freight wagons no longer grind their way up the slopes of Palmer Mountain and the stagecoaches don't make their runs in from Conconully or Ruby, but the Loomis district still draws those who are intrigued by history and fascinated by ruins from the past.

The main street of Loomis, lined with false-front buildings, in those days when Loomis was a bustling and rich mining camp.
(photograph - Courtesy Okanogan County Historical Society)

MOLSON

George B. Mechem was a real booster - and when he advertised he didn't mind stretching the truth.

MOLSON Okanogan WASHINGTON
County

The Gateway to the Colville Indian Reservation
The Land of the Farmer and the Prospector

Thousands of acres of rich land open to the homesteader
Hills filled with GOLD and copper ore ....
Placer in every creek ... for information write
Geo. B. Mechem - Manager
Colville Reservation Syndicates
Molson, Wash.

His advertisement was like many others coming out of the Okanogan country around the turn of the century when the name Molson was acting like a magnet for prospectors and homesteaders. And it had its effect

A birds eye view of Molson when it was on the rise - circa 1910.
(photograph - Courtesy Okanogan County Historical Society)

The Hotel Tonasket in Old Molson. This magnificent building later fell victim to fire. (photograph - Okanogan County Historical Society)

The original telephone company building in New Molson in 1988. Nearly a dozen original buildings survive on the three sites today.

A brass sign proclaiming the "Molson State Bank," adorns the front of the original bank building in Old Molson today. For years Molson was a going concern, considered by its boosters destined to become the great metropolis of the Okanogan Highlands. Alas, fate intervened and Molson, like many western mining towns, slowly withered and eventually died.

A six dollar banknote from Molson's Bank. The Molsons, a noted Canadian banking and brewing family, provided the initial financial backing for the town's founder so the town was named "Molson" in their honor.

because by 1900 the region was teeming with homesteaders, prospectors and boomers. Named after its backer, a wealthy Canadian named John B. Molson, it was touted far and wide. After all, there was farming land to spare, thousands of acres of it; mines like the Poland China and a dozen other prospects and the railroad was coming.

Indeed all of these claims were true and by 1900 Molson claimed a population of 300. With its growing business district and its ½ mile circular race track things seemed to be going as expected. After the magnificent three story Tonasket Hotel was built the pace picked up.

After the railroad finally arrived it quickened. But a land dispute threw ownership of the town lots into question and after a great legal battle about half of the businesses picked up and moved to a new site about half a mile north. Thus "New Molson" came into being. Some of the businesses in Old Molson, including the bank, were able to circumvent the law by being advantageously placed on skids, moving when things got too hot.

In 1914 the population demanded a school. The warring factions in the two towns solved the problem by building the huge school building precisely half way between Old Molson and New Molson. When a number of families and businesses moved to the central location it became known as "Center Molson."

Today the remains of the three Molsons still stand forlornly on their old sites in the Okanogan Highlands; lasting reminders of those years when Molson was the only three site town in the state.

A view of a few of the buildings in Old Molson today.

NIGHTHAWK

It's in the middle of a region once known as the Great American Desert and it is a compelling and unforgettable area. Some ranchers, like the Lintons, the Allemandes and a few other old time families have held fast in their domains in this country, and that is not difficult to understand.

You could wander through this part of the Okanogan for a lifetime and never see it all. It's an enclave from another century and almost unchanged since the time of "Okanogan" Smith.

Drive west from Oroville sometime, past historic Shanker's Bend, then on past historic Rich Bar, follow the abandoned Great Northern right-of-way and the Similkameen river into the heart of the valley. Eventually, where the valley widens, you'll see a cluster of weathered buildings close by the river's edge. This quaint little stopping place has been there since the turn of the century, basking in anonymity for more than half that time.

This is Nighthawk. Once that name was well known, but so were old mines with names like Caaba Lead, California, Mountain Sheep, Golden Zone, Six Eagle and a dozen more that were close by in those days.

Some of the buildings on the historic Caaba mine property just west of old Nighthawk. This mine is now called the Caaba-Texas and is one of the best preserved mines in the county.

The original Nighthawk Hotel, a survivor of the early days of this historic stopping place, still stands in old Nighthawk. This part of western Okanogan County abounds with old mines, decades old buildings, trails, ranches, landmarks and a host of other fascinating reminders of the west of yesterday.

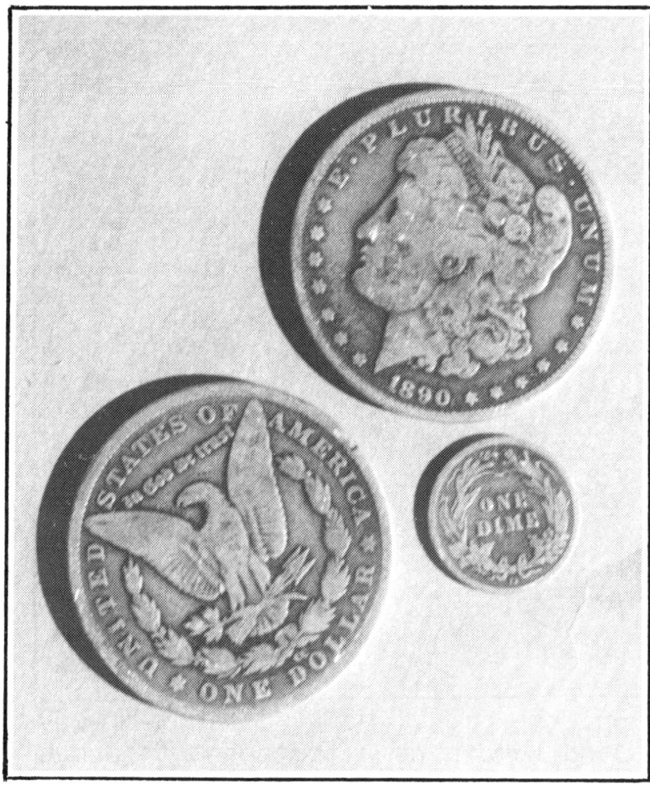

Three of several hundred 1890s silver coins found cached in a hiding place in an old store in historic Nighthawk.

Nighthawk came into being when that country in the northwestern corner of Okanogan County was a beacon for prospectors. With Oroville to the east and Loomis to the southwest, and some spectacular mineral finds in between those two centers, it was not long before a stopping place called "Nighthawk" grew up around a ferry crossing just to the east of Miner's Bend, in the heart of the mineral belt.

By the time the Great Northern subsidiary, the V. V. & E., had laid its track through the valley in 1908, Nighthawk was waiting. By 1910, there was a general store, a railroad station, the Nighthawk Hotel, a saloon with an added attraction of several "girls," and three or four other buildings, all serving the varied requirements of its increasing clientele.

Although the mining eventually subsided, Nighthawk survived. And down through the decades it has remained almost exactly as it was in 1910. True, grizzled prospectors search no more through those barren and strangely beautiful hills in the numbers they once did, but their legacy may still be seen; ore dumps of long dead mines cascading down the mountainsides, long abandoned and weathered buildings and deserted workings. The forlorn and haunting whistle of the Great Northern no longer echoes along the valley as it once did, but those spectacular mountains to the west still stand starkly against the skyline and on its old location Nighthawk still presides - almost unchanged.

Although the rail has been taken up, the old V. V. & E. right-of-way and the tunnel through Shanker's Bend remain as a testament to James J. Hill, the "Empire Builder" of the Great Northern.

OKANOGAN CITY

This old mining camp on the Similkameen river claimed a shifting and brief population of more than 2,000 placer miners in 1860, at the height of the Rich Bar excitement. The exact location of the original site of the camp has never been determined although it was reportedly on the north side of the Similkameen, somewhere between Nighthawk and Shanker's Bend.

Like most temporary placer mining camps, it was primarily a tent town that lasted only a few hectic months. After that rush subsided, however, there were few permanent remains left and little to indicate where it had once stood.

In the State Archives at Olympia, there is an old map that shows a mining camp in the vicinity, but that camp was a lode mining camp of the 1890s, called "Miners' Bend," a different name, upriver and west of Nighthawk, far from the center of the placer activity and mines.

Strangely, although this historic placer camp was the greatest of all of the old placer camps in early Washington, the original site of Okanogan City has never been found. A handful of old silver coins and a few early mining tools have been recovered in the area, but nothing definative. Undoubtedly the site still lies somewhere along the north side of the river - truly a vanished camp from another century.

Somewhere along this stretch of the Similkameen River stood Okanogan City in the early 1860s. It vanished after the gold petered out.

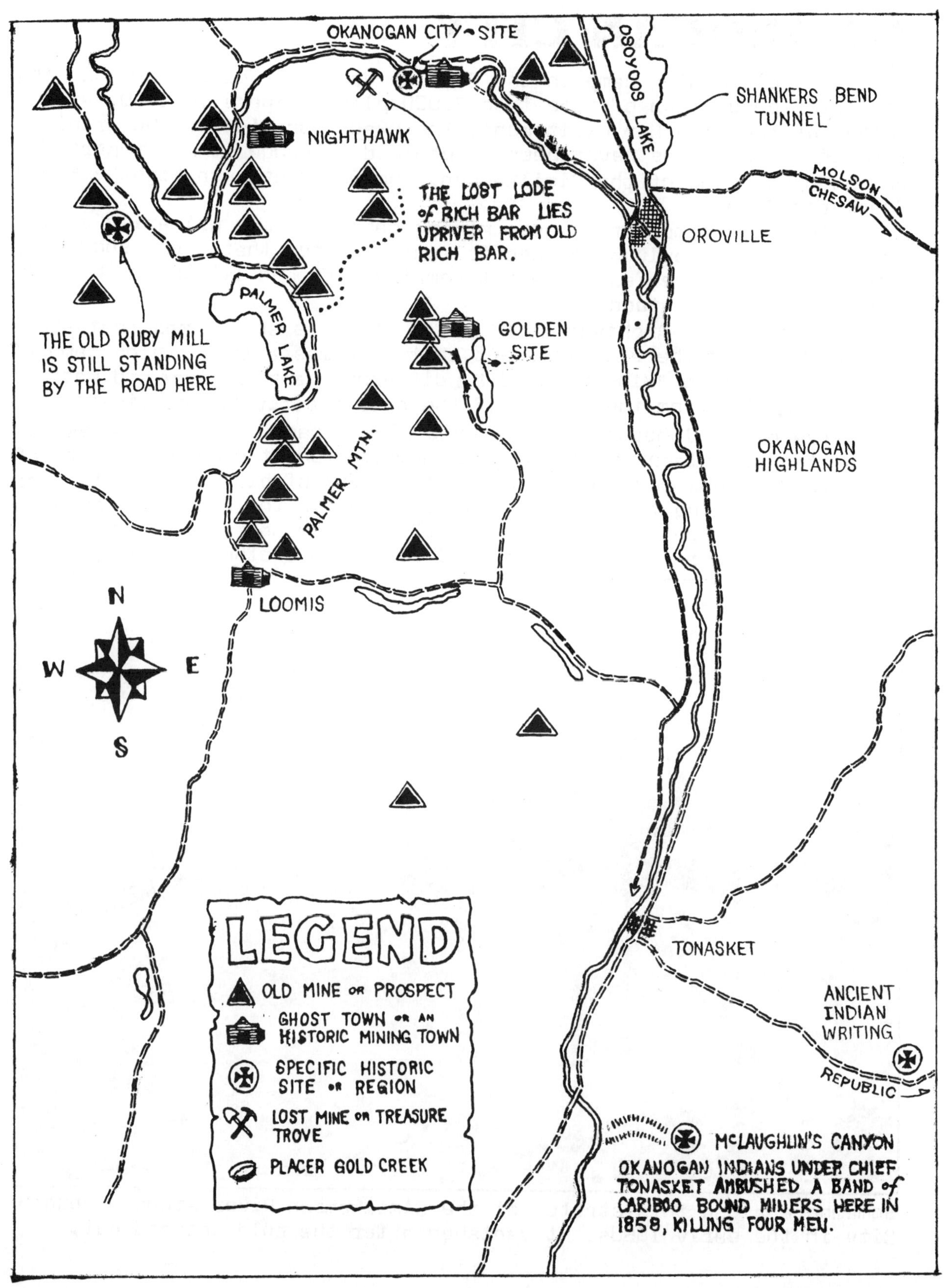
OKANOGAN CITY SITE
OSOYOOS LAKE
SHANKERS BEND TUNNEL
NIGHTHAWK
THE LOST LODE of RICH BAR LIES UPRIVER FROM OLD RICH BAR.
MOLSON
CHESAW
OROVILLE
PALMER LAKE
THE OLD RUBY MILL IS STILL STANDING BY THE ROAD HERE
GOLDEN SITE
OKANOGAN HIGHLANDS
PALMER MTN.
LOOMIS
N
W
E
S
LEGEND
OLD MINE OR PROSPECT
GHOST TOWN OR AN HISTORIC MINING TOWN
SPECIFIC HISTORIC SITE OR REGION
LOST MINE OR TREASURE TROVE
PLACER GOLD CREEK
TONASKET
ANCIENT INDIAN WRITING
REPUBLIC
McLAUGHLIN'S CANYON
OKANOGAN INDIANS UNDER CHIEF TONASKET AMBUSHED A BAND of CARIBOO BOUND MINERS HERE IN 1858, KILLING FOUR MEN.

RUBY

An eerie silence pervades where the main street once stood - and it takes imagination to visualize that a boom town once inhabited the flat. It was called a "city" then, and it was one of the roughest and most talked about mining camps in all of Okanogan County.

Its future was unlimited - like most mining towns. It seemed that the surrounding hills were studded with high grade properties. Silver was found in the area in 1886 on the slopes of both Ruby Mountain and Peacock Hill. By 1887 a Mining District was created and before long a boisterous mining camp grew up beside a creek called the Salmon. With prospectors streaming in to the new find, the population quickly shot up to 700. By 1888 almost seventy buildings were strung out on either side of the main street and the camp, first known simply as Ruby, was calling itself "Ruby City." By the following year it was declared the County Seat and the sky was the limit. With famous mines like the First Thought, Arlington, Fourth of July, Ruby and others spewing out some of the richest silver ore in the state; some of it yielding more than 1,000 ounces per ton, the camp took on a positively cosmopolitan air. The weekly RUBY MINER advertised its mineral riches far and wide, and

Ruby, Washington - circa 1894. This remarkable photograph shows part of the main street of the old mining camp when it was still booming.
(photograph - Courtesy Okanogan County Historical Society)

was confidently predicted that Ruby would soon be vying with Spokane as the mining center of the interior. But later that year Salmon City, an upstart mining town only four miles north of Ruby, whose name had been changed to Conconully, challenged for the County Seat. After the votes had been counted, Conconully had become the new County Seat.

More bad news was to follow. The ore, so rich at the surface and on the upper levels, following what would become an Okanogan pattern, dropped drastically in values at the lower levels. And finally, when the depression of 1893 caused silver prices to plummet, Ruby, like so many other mining camps in the state, was essentially finished.

In a few months the camp lay almost deserted, only a handful of die-hards staying on to salvage what they could from the carnage. The once busy operations on Ruby Mountain and Peacock Hill gradually came to a halt as the bucket tramway from the First Thought ran no longer, and the miners, out of work, drifted on to more promising areas.

Now Ruby City is no more than a memory; the original townsite is barely recognizeable today as nature has reclaimed that once busy flat. Hughie McCool's strange Wooloo Mooloo mine, like most of the others in the vicinity, lies abandoned and forgotten. And those old-timers, who once proudly boasted they they were in "Ruby in 1889," are long gone. And so is Ruby City.

Conconully, pictured here, challenged Ruby for supremacy of Okanogan county in the 1890s and became the County Seat. The historic mining camp of Ruby faded and vanished soon after.

TWISP

Twisp doesn't look like an old mining town now, but it was once. In those years mines like the Red Shirt, Pride of the Hills, Brooklyn, Black Warrior and half a dozen others barely three miles east of the forks of the Methow and Twisp rivers, gave rise to a short-lived camp called Silver. Silver soon vanished but when other mineral discoveries were made far up the Twisp, on both Gilbert and Goat Park Mountains, a supply point called Twisp came into being.

When Silver was virtually wiped out by the flood of 1894, Twisp, which escaped the brunt of the high water, began to prosper. Soon its streets were clogged with prospectors heading up the Twisp or farther north, into the Slate Creek Mining District, or fanning out in other directions, looking for El Dorado.

And Twisp grew considerably. It was on the stagecoach run and it was on the map. Its business district was really quite impressive, as concerns like the Commercial Bank, the Spokane Store, Burke Brothers, the White Front Cafe, M. C. Alsabrook and dozens of other businesses, large and small, established there.

And Twisp is still standing at the confluence of the Methow and the Twisp, the lone survivor of the three mining camps of the past.

Glover Street in Twisp around 1909. Twisp was busy and booming in the first decade of the century when mines like the Red Shirt were going.
(photograph - Courtesy Eastern Washington State Historical Society)

Early morning in old Twisp

Children running down the main street of Twisp to watch as the Twisp brass band swings into action - circa 1915.
(Photographs - courtesy of the Okanogan County Historical Society)

WAUCONDA

The first Wauconda came into being in 1898, after the three Hedges brothers discovered a wide ledge of quartz carrying free gold in it. This find was located on a summit nearly three miles west of Clackamas Mountain. This discovery touched off a headlong rush into the area as prospectors envisioned another Eureka Camp.

By 1898 a considerable community had grown up around the mine. A wagon road soon connected the property to Republic and before long a general store, three crude hotels, four saloons and a handful of other businesses catered to the miners needs. By 1901, a post office opened with Morton Hill as the first postmaster; and Wauconda was finally on the map. With enterprising businessmen like Fred Gugat, J. R. VanSlyke and several others, the camp soon claimed a population of 300. It was a thriving place in those first years with Jack Thorp's stage running from Chesaw to Republic twice a week and always rattling to a stop in Wauconda to disgorge passengers or pick up mail.

By 1901, however, the mine was showing signs of depletion as the ore began piching out. Soon after it closed down, sounding the death knell for the original town. But its inhabitants, refusing to abandon the district, simply picked up and moved westward to a new site about

The picturesque Pflug mansion south of Wauconda. Tucked into a grassy draw close by the highway, most passersby don't even see this historic old house.

two miles away. The second Wauconda never really matched the status of its predecessor. It did have a school, a post office, several places of business and a growing population of homesteaders, but it never did approach "town" status. And when the new highway between Republic and Tonasket bypassed the second town in 1929, its stock plummeted and it was predicted that it too would soon vanish. But J. R. VanSlyke, still determined to keep the name alive, picked up stakes in 1930 and moved his store and post office to a new site close by the highway. So the last Wauconda stands yet by Highway 20 and not too far away from the original sites.

Wauconda today doesn't resemble that camp of the past, but it is the center of one of the most compelling regions in Okanogan County. In every direction history beckons. To the north lie old mining camps like Bodie, Old Toroda and Sheridan and scores of abandoned mines and prospects and puzzling landmarks like Corkscrew Mountain. To the east is Republic and Ferry County and to the southwest the Indian country of the ever remembered Bonaparte Creek valley with its ancient Indian campsites, historic trails and Indian pictographs. And close by "new" Wauconda may be found scores of abandoned log cabins and old deserted houses, including that haunting derelict; the old Pflug mansion. It's an area where the memories run deep and the past is at your shoulder.

One of many abandoned log cabins in the Wauconda region. This part of Okanogan county is captivating for all those interested in history.

WINTHROP

The old Winthrop brass band doesn't parade down the main street as it once did, and Guy Waring and Col. Tom Hart no longer frequent their old haunts. And you can't hear the rumble of the freight wagons as they wend their way westward. Even those pure metal men of old are no more than a memory.

But there was a time when this town was sure fire. In the 1890s, it was booming and Winthrop was transferred from being a little known stopping place to a bustling distribution point. Like most of Okanogan County in those years, mining activity was the fuse that ignited its growth. When an eccentric named Guy Waring established a trading post at the forks of the Methow and Chewack rivers in 1891, he found himself on the very edge of the frontier. Beyond, to the north and west, lay the Cascades, a formidable barrier.

But good fortune soon attended the trader. In the spring of 1868 placer gold had been discovered in the Slate Creek District in nearby Whatcom County by Thomas Keefe, William Milliken and Joshua Hardy. Although the placer discoveries drew hundreds of miners into the new district, it was the later discoveries of lode mines which kept them

Winthrop, Washington, probably around 1910. Winthrop was fairly well established by then thanks to nearby mining activity.
(Photograph - Courtesy Okanogan County Historical Society)

there. By the 1890s, with prospectors pouring into the region, mainly from Okanogan County, Winthrop gradually assumed the role of staging point. And when the indomitable Colonel, Tom Hart, built a magnificent road the 34 miles into Slate Creek, its future was guaranteed.

Farther up the Methow places like Mazama and Robinson came into their own when mineral finds were made in those areas. But the mining era, like all mining eras, too quickly came to an end. By 1915 most of the mines, except for a few in the Slate Creek area, had closed down. Winthrop was hard hit and it gradually declined in importance as its population plummeted. It struggled through the depression years amidst rumors that it was destined to become a ghost town. But Winthrop hung on through the tough times and emerged intact; even its main street was almost unchanged, rare in a western mining town.

Now Mazama is barely more than a name. Robinson has vanished and the once famous Slate Creek District lies abandoned and neglected. But Harts original wagon road can still be traced in places today, especially that section that winds along the cliff faces up to the 6,000' Harts Pass and then drops down into the gloomy Slate Creek area.

And Winthrop - Winthrop is alive and well and prospering. The old town has been restored and a surprising number of original buildings still stand along its main street. The old Duck Brand Saloon is gone and so is Guy Waring, but Winthrop has retained that mood of old.

Knights of Pythias parade along the main street of Winthrop somewhere around 1905. (Courtesy Okanogan County Historical Society)

PLACER GOLD

A thousand dollars worth of "lead" gold which was recovered by the author and his partner in 1986. This type of placer gold was typical of the gold mined at famous Rich Bar on the Similkameen River when that renowned and amazingly rich spot drew placer miners from all over the West during the late 1850s and early 1860s.

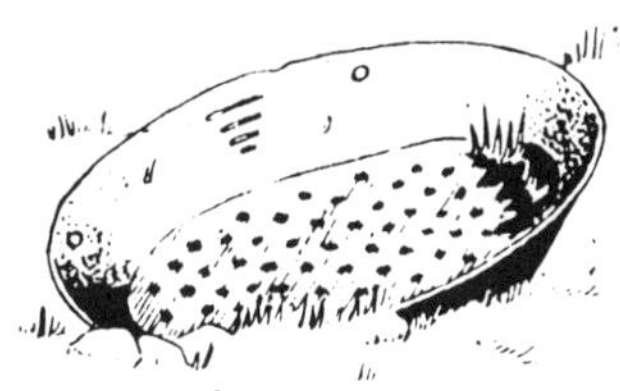

Mary Ann Creek ● Discovered to be gold bearing by 1896 and possibly somewhat earlier. Mary Ann had produced an estimated 3,000 ounces of placer gold since its discovery, 2,400 ounces from 1896 to 1906, and 600 ounces since then, mainly from 1930s operations like the Johnston, Ottia May, Spoonamore and a handful of others. The gold is sometimes, but not always, rusty colored and often coarse, with nuggets of up to ½ ounce or more. The gold occurs on both bedrock and on a clay seam, or false bedrock, about 4' above true bedrock. The larger nuggets may have quartz attached to them, a peculiarity which lends credibility to the theory that the origin of the gold is close by, probably from the north side of the creek somewhere near the North Fork junction.

Prospects: Mary Ann still deserves a long look. A systematic search could reveal the source of the gold which peters out shortly upstream and above the mouth of the North Fork. This placer creek still yields good colors in every pan at selected locations. It is a renowned gold creek with a fascinating past and good possibilities, even today. The ranchers in the area control this creek and any mining proposals would have to go through them.

This painting of an early day prospector indicates the trials and general difficulties pioneer prospectors faced in the far west. In early Washington Territory virtually every creek and river through the entire state was prospected for 'colors' or other indications, or signs of placer gold.

Methow River ● The mouth of this important waterway is located at Pateros on the Columbia river. The Methow drains a large area which is fairly well mineralized, especially in its upper reaches. In the 1890s there was sporadic activity along the Methow, especially on the part of the river northwest of old Winthrop. Some fine gold has been recovered below the mouths of tributaries like Wolf, Goat and Early Winters creeks. The gold is almost uniformly fine.

Prospects: Again a fine gold river with sparsely scattered gold deposits along its upper parts. The Methow river is not considered to be good placer ground and it has been well prospected.

Myers Creek ● This creek in the Chesaw area has yielded an unknown amount of placer gold since the 1890s. The gold is much finer and less plentiful than that found on Mary Ann creek, its more famous tributary. Myers creek was mined by Chinese argonauts for a number of years and they undoubtedly recovered significant quantities of the yellow metal during that time.

Prospects: Although Myers creek has been essentially idle since the 1930s, it has produced some relatively coarse gold so it should not be passed up. Although the Chinese were not noted for missing many paystreaks, it might be worthwhile prospecting close to their old workings which are acattered along the stream.

Wheel on Myers Creek near Chesaw at the turn of the century.
(photograph - Courtesy Okanogan County Historical Society)

North Fork Creek ● This branch of Mary Ann creek has probably yielded at least 450 ounces of gold. Most of that production was obtained from the central part of this stream, both from bedrock and higher benches. It was handmined and even hydraulicked around 1896. Some considerable amount of coarse gold and nuggets were recovered. An interrupted old high channel once crossed from one side of this little stream to the opposite side. Some rimrock has been worked. In dry years, the water is extremely low and may hamper operations.

Prospects: Interesting. This creek deserves a harder look. Try the benches high above the creek, especially close to the original mining site almost a mile from the mouth.

Salmon Creek ● This creek runs through the old town of Conconully in the west central part of Okanogan County. The Salmon has long been a producer of placer gold. Discovered to be gold bearing in the 1880s, it was a fairly steady but never spectacular producer. The gold tends to be fairly fine with occasional small nuggets. Some of the original claims downstream from Conconully are now inundated by the waters of the Conconully Reservoir. Probably the best producing ground today is located about seven or eight miles northwest of old Conconully on the north fork of Salmon creek. Some of the placer gold was nuggety in the early years but is invariably fine today.

This blurry photograph - c 1896, shows an hydraulic operation on the North Fork of Mary Ann creek. (Okanogan County Historical Society)

Prospects: Not encouraging although the north fork section yields a certain amount of fine gold. The possibilities of finding an ancient channel along the north fork is remote but not impossible. Other gold creeks in Okanogan County, however, hold far greater promise.

Similkameen River ● One of the great placer gold rivers of the state. This waterway gained its reputation when a relatively short section of the river yielded over 31,000 ounces of gold. In September of 1859 a detachment of soldiers under the command of Capt. J. J. Archer of the Boundary Survey, discovered gold on a bar of the river. The October 21, 1859, issue of the DALLES JOURNAL, contained this extract:

> New and Rich Gold Discoveries on the Si-mil-ka-meen River
>
> An expressman, named McGuire, arrived at the Dalles in the early part of the week from Captain Archer's command, reports the discovery of rich gold diggings on the Si-mil-ka-meen river, about five miles from the camp. According to our informant, the discovery is confined to a small bar on the

The Similkameen river wending eastward at Shanker's Bend, between old Nighthawk and Oroville. Most of the river looks the same as it did in 1859 when soldiers came across staggeringly rich placer gold.

> river, which is being worked by soldiers, quartermaster's men, and a large number of Indians. The men from camp go down after breakfast, walking a distance of about five miles, and working not more than half a day, average about $20 to the hand. This is without the ordinary conveniences of mining, and with nothing but picks, using frying pans for washing out ... The Indians, too, are represented to be decidedly hostile; and inasmuch as the troops are about to remove, miners would be exposed to constant attacks from savage foes. We mention these facts as a caution against a wild and headlong rush, ... The discovery ... was made by Sergeant Compton in whose honour the locality has been named "Compton Bar."

On October 8, 1859, Captain J.J. Archer wrote a short letter to the PIONEER and DEMOCRAT which contained the following information:

The Okanogan Indians were hostile during the late 1850s. In 1858, under the leadership of Tonasket, a renegade chief, they ambushed a party of miners northward bound under the command of one John McLaughlin. In the ensuing battle four miners were killed and the remainder were forced to parlay with the shrewd Tonasket. This photograph was taken looking southwest from McLaughlin's Canyon.

I am detached with 14 men at the N. W. B. station on the Si-mil-ka-meen, about 12 miles from its mouth .... On the 6th, my sergeant showed me the result of six pans which he washed and we found to be worth $6. On the 7th, two men obtained $20 each; others from $5 to $15. We have no tools or conveniences, and the men know little about digging gold. I give you the simple facts .... It is much coarser gold than any found on Fraser River, some pieces weighing $2 to $50....

Captain J. J. Archer's letter mentions that some pieces weighing up to $50 were recovered by his soldiers. This indicates the coarseness of the gold because the standard payment for raw placer gold in 1859 was $16 a troy ounce. So a $50 slug would have weighed just over three ounces troy, and with twelve ounces to a troy pound, those nuggets were over a quarter of a pound in weight.

Most sources estimate that $500,000 in gold was recovered from the Similkameen; most of that from "Rich Bar" and immediately downstream.

Just over 100 ounces of coarse gold and nuggets mined by the writer and his partner in 1986 on a branch of the Similkameen on the Canadian side of the line. Valued at nearly $50,000, this gold is known as "lead" gold and is part of 518 ounces recovered from a section of an old and long buried channel - proof that ancient channels are often extremely rich.

The river was worked heavily from 1859 onward, and the majority of the gold was recovered between 1859 and 1899 although the river has been mined intermittently ever since, first by snipers, and in the last twenty years by dredgers.

Prospects: Although the Similkameen has produced many thousands of ounces of gold to generations of placer men, the once productive bedrock has been generally well mined and only isolated spots will yield pay today. Placer miners should consider the possibilities of the existence of ancient, buried channels on the flats and benches on the north side of the river in the Rich Bar area.

Toroda Creek ● This stream rises in eastern Okanogan County and flows first through that county and then into Ferry County before it joins the Kettle river. Although not a noted placer gold producer it wends through mining country and has yielded small amounts of generally fine gold. It was thoroughly prospected in the 1890s but has never been more than a fitful and desultory producer since that time. The lower part of the creek downstream from Old Toroda is easy to prospect although bedrock is difficult to find.

Prospects: A pleasant and interesting stream to prospect but the chances of making a good find are slim indeed.

The scenic Similkameen river wends its way through the valley of the Similkameen. Some abandoned placer mining equipment lies in the foreground of this once noted placer gold river.

Twisp River ● This river flows into the Methow from the west and has produced some flour gold from several locations along its route. The majority of this placer gold was recovered from claims at the junction of South creek and the Twisp. Both the mouths of War creek and Little Bridge creek have also yielded some fine gold. The placers at the mouth of South creek were mined during the late 1880s but the production was never recorded.

Prospects: The Twisp never had bonanza ground and it is considered to be a "lean" river today. It's a scenic river to prospect but don't expect much more than flour gold.

The deserted camp of Gilbert on the Twisp River as it looked in 1909. In those days the Twisp region was highly touted as mining country as disocveries had been made in all directions. This photograph by C. R. Lewis, a local photographer, not only captured the mood of an abandoned mining camp, but other details as well. The unidentified prospector in the foreground has prospecting tools and a Colt revolver, typical and almost mandatory equipment for the time. In the photograph the cabins are still in relatively good condition, suggesting that they had been used, probably as a jumping-off point for the many prospectors in the region who were constantly scouring the area close by in their never ending search for bonanza ore.

TREASURES & LOST MINES

Looking westward and up the Similkameen River, with Rich Bar Rock in the foreground. Somewhere close by, perhaps under the rolling hills visible in the photograph, lies the long sought after "Rich Bar Vein."

THE LOST LODE OF RICH BAR

When Rich Bar on the Similkameen was discovered in 1859, the gold recovered there was both plentiful and coarse, with some of the nuggets tilting the scales at a quarter of a pound. Although the entire length of the river, from its mouth to the Canadian line, was prospected, only one section was found to be gold bearing - Rich Bar. Over 31,000 ounces; a total of more than 2,500 pounds troy, came from that locality, mainly from Rich Bar itself, with diminishing amounts recovered downriver from that celebrated spot.

It was an astonishing find but some of those early prospectors, the experienced hands, knew that the origin of the gold lay very close by. By the late 1890s, serious attempts to locate the motherlode were being made. These men, most of them old hard rock miners, knew that there was a vein or series of veins just upriver from Rich Bar - and these veins had been the origin of the massive amounts of coarse placer gold which

The original Linton cabin on the flats north of the Similkameen River and Rich Bar. Many parts of the country in this section of the county are reminiscent of the early West; sagebrush, desert, abandoned mines and long deserted buildings.

had been recovered by earlier miners.

In 1901, a prospector named Charles Peterson came across several quartz stringers. Convinced that he had found the motherlode he sank two shafts, certain that he would tap untold riches at depth. At the 50 foot and 150 foot levels of the deepest shaft he drifted. Finally, at 150 feet he hit an ore body striking north 50 degrees west and dipping 35 to 40 degrees northeast. It was a massive 6 foot wide ore body with a lode material of bluish-white quartz enclosed in a quartzite slate. Unfortunately, the vein varied considerably in mineral content, usually assaying only a disappointing "trace" of gold, and only infrequently as high as two ounces per ton. By and large, the vein was not worth pursuing although Peterson, and several others, did form a mining company called the Rich Bar Mining Company, but only some desultory and rather disappointing work was done thereafter on his eleven claims, and they were finally allowed to lapse.

A handful of miners who were familiar with the area were convinced that the vein Peterson found in 1901 was not the Rich Bar vein, that it was simply too low grade, and that he missed the incredibly rich gold bearing vein that he was searching for. And in all probability they are correct in this assumption because well over a ton of coarse gold has been recovered, mainly on Rich Bar - and that gold must have originated upriver and just beyond that historic bar. The old theory that it had broken away from a hidden vein and had been carried downriver many eons ago and had lodged just downstream on Rich Bar is generally accepted.

So, somewhere along that scenic river they call the Similkameen, west of Shanker's Bend and Rich Bar, lies a fabulously rich vein. It's quite possible that someone will find it one day, but that individual will require unusual diligence and good fortune because the vein must lie below the level of the river and thus be hidden from view. But the "Lost Lode of Rich Bar," assuredly does exist and still awaits discovery, somewhere just upstream from that abandoned bar which, so many decades ago, echoed to the sound of placer miners.

II
FERRY COUNTY

INTRODUCTION

Ferry County - The roaring days have vanished and so have the glory years of the mining era in this historic county. But in those towns like old Republic, Orient, Curlew and half a dozen other places, the echoes of bonanza days and bonanza times can still be faintly heard. Riders on lathered horses no longer pound down the dusty main street of Republic as they did so many Fourth of July days almost a century ago and the steady pounding of stamp mills no longer reverberates in the hills as it once did, but this is still mining country where old names like Knob Hill, Morning Star, Surprise, Quilp, Lone Pine and a hundred other mines conjure up visions of iron men, gold and silver.

Alas, men with nicknames like "Long Alec," "Lightning Bill" and "Powderkeg Pete" are long gone from their old haunts but in the north, in the border country, little has changed. That memorable river they call the Kettle presides yet over those rolling hills, flowing past deserted Ferry, then Curlew and Danville and over the Canadian line before doubling back in a great arc to join the Columbia.

On the Colville Indian Reservation, far to the south, Inchelium, Keller and other little known places still provide a window into the early west - as does much of this country known as Ferry County.

Keller when it was young. It never really got off the ground as a lode mining center although there are many showings in the district.
(photograph - Courtesy Eastern Washington State Historical Society)

BELCHER CAMP

The name Belcher Camp is seldom heard today, even in Ferry County. There were scores of more important mining camps in the state during its heyday but few were as unique as Belcher. Its population, even at its height was only 75 souls and it wasn't even a gold camp, its miners mined iron - definitely a second class metal compared to gold.

It was located on upper Lambert creek, nearly ten miles northeast of Republic. When a large body of high grade iron ore was discovered in the vicinity around 1897, the Belcher Mountain Mining Company began operations soon after. By 1906 the camp was the complete mining camp, relying only on its own resources. With a population of between 60 and 75 people it was centered around a post office, a large bunkhouse for single miners, a general store, five or six houses - and a railroad.

And of all the railroad lines in the state, past and present, the Belcher Mountain Railroad was probably the most unusual. Built initially to haul ore from the Belcher mine to ore bunkers just north of Karamin, this little narrow gauge line only eight miles long, soon doubled as a passenger carrier. When someone at the mine wanted to go to Republic, the crew simply hooked a passenger car on behind the ore cars and that individual would be taken down the line, riding regally and alone, to make connections with the Washington and Northern to complete the last leg of the trip to Republic. It had the niceties of larger railroads too. Ed Williams, the conductor, had a three man crew including a brakeman, a fireman and even a condcutor. Eventually the mine folded, the camp was abandoned and the line disappeared. Today there isn't much left to mark their passing - the Belcher Mountain Railroad is no more.

CURLEW

Late in 1896, soon after the opening up of the "North Half" of the Colville Indian Reservation to mineral entry, two enterprising traders, Guy S. Helphry and J. Walters, set up a general store at an old ferry crossing near the junction of Curlew creek and the Kettle river. This trading post quickly burgeoned into a collection of log buildings and stores. By 1901 a bridge spanned the Kettle and the community, with a population of nearly 200, claimed two general stores, two saloons, a hotel, two livery stables, a dry goods store and several other houses of business. A post office had been established in 1898 and the town was designated "Curlew."

Those early years were banner times for Curlew as the region was flooded with prospectors, mining magnates, railroad workers, Indians, freighters and the usual flotsam attracted to a new frontier. Nearby, mines like the Drummer, Lancaster and Panama were touted as the great new El Dorados.

But Curlew, unlike Republic, never really got off the ground. It seemed to stand still after those heady first years. The mineral belt,

A rare early view of Curlew's business section somewhere around 1905. In those days Curlew was a center for prospectors, mining magnates and railroad men. (courtesy Eastern Washington State Historical Society)

An early photograph of Curlew showing the Great Northern train pulling into town. (courtesy Eastern Washington State Historical Society)

The old Ansorge Hotel as it appears today.

once so widely acclaimed, failed to live up to those early expectations, so the dreams of Curlew as another great mining center of Ferry County slowly faded.

But Curlew still stands on that bench overlooking the Kettle, in one of the most picturesque settings in the county. The Ansorge Hotel is still there although many of its older false-fronted buildings no longer line its streets and Indians like the famous "Long Alex" have vanished from the local scene, but in many places, just out of town, or along the Kettle, or deep in the high country, it hasn't changed a bit.

Danville around 1909. It was a busy camp in those days, with both gold and silver being produced by the mines in the vicinity.
(photograph - Courtesy Helen Brinkman)

DANVILLE

This place is rarely mentioned in the mining annals of the state although it ranks in the forefront of historic mining camps in Ferry County, surpassed only by Republic. Its mines, some of which produced impressive amounts of high grade ore, shipped their product northward into British Columbia to smelters in Grand Forks or Greenwood in the famous Boundary Country, and few records of their production during the years between 1898 and 1938 have survived.

Danville lies just south of the border and was the first town in the county. First known as "Nelson," it was established in 1889 by the Nelson brothers, after whom the settlement was named. In late 1896 it became the jumping off place for prospectors impatiently waiting for the "North Half" of the Colville Indian Reservation to be opened up. By 1897 it had half a dozen businesses, a post office and the first newspaper in the county - the RESERVATION RECORD. In this same year, the Nelson brothers, ever ready to take advantage of the mining boom taking place on both sides of the line, built a commodious store right on the International Boundary Line with a north entrance and a south entrance; the former to serve customers from Canada, the latter for their United States patrons. Unfortunately, the authorities, suspecting customs duty evasion, closed the store and it was taken back soon after to Nelson.

In 1901, when the Washington & Great Northern Railroad, part of the Great Northern empire, built through Nelson their officials had the name changed to "Danville" to avoid confusion with Nelson in British Columbia, a great mining town in the West Kootenay District. By then, mines like the Morning Star, Lucille Dreyfus, Surprise and a handful

A birdseye view of Danville, probably around 1910 when the mines were still producing and the town was prospering.

(photograph - Courtesy Helen Brinkman)

of others were shipping quantities of gold, silver and copper ores to smelters across the line.

While the mines were running Danville prospered, but eventually the ore pinched out, the mines closed and Danville, hard hit, slipped in importance as activity waned. During the 1920s some measure of prosperity returned with prohibition. Danville, like Nighthawk, Chesaw and Molson in Okanogan County, became a smugglers rendezvous. As a variety of old trails and roads suddenly came into use again, some much needed cash changed hands as the whiskey smugglers used local guides to avoid the customs patrols guarding the border. When prohibition finally came to an end, Danville entered a long decline. As the years passed the face of the town changed as a series of fires took their deadly toll. And those characters of the early days, like old man Jennings, who in his spare time, it was rumored, augmented his slim income as a Justice of the Peace, by counterfeiting half dollars, moved on.

Today Danville still occupies that spacious flat where "Nelson" was first established so long ago, but it has changed. There are only two original buildings still standing in the old business section, but across the Kettle River, somewhere in those hills beyond, the "Lost Golden Plate Ledge" lies hidden, awaiting discovery.

A Fourth of July parade in old Danville - circa 1920. In those years the town was still dreaming dreams of glory but Danville soon faded.
(photograph - Courtesy Helen Brinkman)

FERRY

The Canadians used to say that Ferry was "The toughest town this side of Hell!" And maybe they were right because Ferry did have a bad reputation, especially during the late 1890s. There was a rough set of characters living in Ferry then; more than a few of them barely a step ahead of the law.

Strangely, although it was a wide open camp with a colorful and sometimes violent history, it is little known outside of the county. It was founded during the late 1890s when British Columbia's Boundary District was booming and great mining towns like Grand Forks, Phoenix and Greenwood were becoming household names in the mining world.

Ferry was thrown up almost overnight, a ramshackle collection of crude log and false-front buildings bordering a dusty main street. It got its share of traffic during those heady years, most of it heading north into British Columbia. But when the mining boom subsided so did Ferry. By 1910 it was on the downward slope as insurance fires took a steady toll and before long Ferry had passed into oblivion.

There is barely a sign of that once busy camp today, occasionally a faintly visible depression on the wind swept flat, or a coin lost so long ago, shows up, then, and ever so momentarily, images of the camp flicker to life - but they are brief because the Ferry of old is gone.

A solitary safe, rusted and forgotten, marks the abandoned site of once prosperous Ferry.

This rare photograph shows Ferry in detail - c 1910. It is one of several ghost towns in the **state that** has seldom been chronicled. (photograph - Courtesy Archives of British Columbia)

ORIENT

A strange name - an interesting background. Sometimes appearances can be misleading, they are in Orient. Today this historic town still overlooks the Kettle river, as it has since it was founded close to a century ago. But the little place of the present is far different than that town of yesterday.

Then, like few other places in Ferry County, outside of booming Republic, it was considered a sure thing; the coming metropolis of the north country. In those days some of its boosters, and there were many then, claimed that it would eventually surpass even Republic as the greatest mining camp in the county. And for awhile it looked as though their boasts might come true.

When three prospectors; Maloney, Morris and Dunkle discovered the Never Tell mine, a startlingly rich deposit of free milling gold ore, it ignited a stampede into the region. In quick succession a series of other discoveries were made on First Thought Hill and Toulou Mountain, just across the river from a temporary camp the miners called "Orient," a name chosen because Oriental placer miners had once mined the bars of the river there decades before, and their abandoned diggingd were still visible by the river's edge.

The main street of Orient in 1910. The mines were situated across the river. (photograph - Eastern Washington State Historical Society)

Within months scores of mines with names like First Thought, New Golden Crown, North Star, Trophy, Orient, Globe, Iron Horse, Pennant, Sure Thing, Defender, Trojan, Paymaster, Last Chance and many others were producing spectacular ore. And the properties radiated out from Orient like the spokes of a wheel.

By 1905 mines like the First Thought, which produced a staggering $180,000 in ore, mainly gold, had put the town on the map. Soon, Main Street began to mirror the new wealth. By 1910, a permanent bridge of more than 300 feet spanned the Kettle, the Orient State Bank was open for business and other amenities like a school, a town hall and even a newspaper; Alex Anderson's KETTLE RIVER JOURNAL, proclaimed to all and sundry that Orient was going places. And it looked like it was.

Unfortunately, there is a direct relationship between the wealth flowing from the mines and a mining town's prosperity - and Orient was no different from a hundred other mining camps of the old West. When it was found that the gold values didn't generally carry to depth, it was the beginning of a long, slow decline. When the newspaper finally ceased publication, the die had been irrevocably cast and one by one, most of the businesses along main street followed suite. By the 1940s, despite occasional flurries of mining activity, Orient was little more than a stopping place.

The face of that old camp has almost disappeared today, but the memories still hover close by. The once humming mines are silent now, but First Thought Hill is still there and so is the Kettle, unchanged since those first miners came into the district almost a century-ago, convinced that Orient was the new El Dorado.

One of the few original buildings still standing in Orient today. But across the Kettle river, history still beckons.

REPUBLIC

It was late February of 1896, possibly too late. It was the 22nd, but the Colville Indian Reservation had been opened for mineral entry the day before - they were a full day late and still nearly a hundred miles from their destination. They were in Rossland, a booming mining town in British Columbia and they were heading for the San Poil creek region, far to the south-west, and it was dead winter.

Their names; Tommy Ryan and Phil Creasor, both tramp prospectors who had been grubstaked by three businessmen from the Inland Empire to check out the rumors that somewhere on the upper San Poil was bonanza ground. Their grubstakers were L. H. Long, C. R. Robbins and a certain James Clark, brother of the famous Patsy Clark, the mining magnate. It was a long shot because other prospectors had started earlier.

Before the day was out they had left Rossland, boarded a Spokane Falls & Northern Railroad train at booming Northport, and headed west. Disembarking at old Bossburg, they purchased outfits and horses in the big mining supplies store, then hurried down the Columbia river, aware that any delay might easily defeat their quest. They turned north-west

Miners in the gold camp of Eureka Gulch in 1897. In February of 1896, the first prospectors in the gulch, Tommy Ryan and Phil Creasor, had come across magnificent ledges of ore and had staked the ground. The camp soon took the name "Republic," and ultimately became one of the greatest gold camps in the west. (Courtesy Dept. of Natural Resources)

at the mouth of the Kettle river and doggedly followed it as it looped back into Canada. It was a long route but it skirted the Kettle River Range, a formidable obstacle of high wilderness and deep snows. On or about February 26th, the Kettle finally led them back into Washington again. Pausing at Nelson (now Danville), a crude frontier outpost near the border, they met another prospector, George Welty. Welty told them that he and his brother John, anxious to be the first into the district, had camped on San Poil creek all winter, impatiently waiting until the area was thrown open. Welty generously invited the other prospectors to return with him to his camp. They arrived at the Welty camp on the 28th of February and early the next morning Creasor and Ryan started out, moving rapidly westward. But as they edged toward their goal, feelings of both expectation and dread attended them - the hope that they would be the first on the ground was balanced by the likelihood that others had already beaten them to it. But as they plodded steadily through the silence and the snows, they gradually realized that although they were a week late, they were the only prospectors in the vicinity, no tell-tale tracks in the snow and an almost eerie silence prevailed.

Finally they noticed a promising looking draw, and a few minutes after entering it they discovered a massive and continuous mineralized

Eureka Gulch around 1908. Pictured are the Mammoth Hill, Black Tail, Lone Pine and Quilp mines. In those days the mines were producing a king's ransom in gold and nearby Republic was alive with activity.
(photograph - Courtesy Ferry County Historical Society)

ledge. The next day, they, along with the Welty brothers, located the Lone Pine, Iron Mask and the Copper Belle. Soon after that, in quick succession the Republic, Quilp, San Poil, Blacktail, Mountain Lion and the Jim Blaine were located. Several others were also staked at the same time, including an afterthought which they casually called Knob Hill.

Although the initial assays were disappointing, later samples gave up to $35.00 a ton in gold. On the strength of the numerous outcrops, high assays and whispers of a great strike, a mining camp gradually began to develop. That first camp in Eureka Gulch, with its collection of tents and log cabins was, like so many other early mining camps of the West, christened "Eureka." And it wasn't long before it rocketed to fame. When the Republic mine hit a bonanza shoot of fabulous ore in late 1896, the camp was on its way.

Soon the entire area was being crossed and criss-crossed as hordes of tramp prospectors gravitated into the new district and thousands of locations were recorded. And when high-rollers like Patsy Clark, the famous brother of Jim Clark, began buying up mines and shares, it was the making of the camp.

The new El Dorado soon changed its name from Eureka to Republic. And in those years it was quite a town. With a population approaching the 2,000 mark it had an impressive and booming business district. By

Looking down Clark Avenue in Republic around 1900. Republic was close to the 2,000 population mark then and growing daily.
(Photograph - Courtesy Eastern Washington State Historical Society)

1900 it had more than 20 saloons; most of them doing a roaring trade, seven hotels, nine general stores, three newspapers, a bank, an opera house and scores of other businesses. Like most mining towns of that day it also had a busy red light district whose "girls" were known by obscure names like "French Marie" or "Holdout Annie" and whose establishments were designed to separate amorous miners from their hard won pay. And when the ladies of the night missed, the gambling emporiums with games like roulette, faro, stud poker or any of a number of other games of chance, seldom failed to separate the unwary from his poke. Even notoriously fortunate gamblers like Patsy Clark on more than one occasion lost hefty stacks of gold coins to the tinhorns.

And there were serious setbacks. On June 3, 1899, a conflagration of epic proportions swept along Clark Avenue and left more than half of the business district in ashes and a staggering $100,000 in losses. Even the use of dynamite in the path of the fire had failed to prevent the inexorable progress of the blaze, which left scores of uninsured businesses bankrupt. Half a dozen mines, especially the great Republic mine, which was producing as many as fifty gold bars a month in this era, were producing significantly but the vast majority; on the edges of the gold belt, were generally no more than sporadic producers even at the best of times so Republic, like other mining towns, was always

John Stack's big store in Republic - circa 1899. The loungers on the boardwalk are probably waiting for the mail to arrive.
(photograph - Courtesy Eastern Washington State Historical Society)

heavily dependent upon the fluctuating fortunes of its mines. By 1910 the town hadn't really changed much; the Fourth of July holiday still attracted 1,500 spectators who lined Clark Avenue to watch the contests and festivities. Those were the days when Bill Galloway came in from Wauconda to pit his horses; Irish Mick and Tim Toulon, against the local favorites; Art May's Lucille and Baptiste Tonasket's Indian cayuses; San Poil Sam and Red Bird. It was winner take all, with thousands of dollars changing hands on the outcome. And it was a colorful town with productions at the opera house and bare knuckle brawls in the saloons, with both of these diverse attractions enthralling considerable and quite different audiences. Republic was still busy then, with both the Spokane & British Columbia; more commonly known as the "Hot Air" line, and the Washington Northern, competing mightily for the lion's share of the ore trade, which by that time was slowly declining in volume and threatening the very existence of the town. In that year, however, an event took place - an event which ultimately proved to be the greatest benefit that the town had ever received. Almost unheralded a virtually unknown mine called the Knob Hill came into production. Somehow this property had been ignored for almost a decade and a half but before a dozen years had passed it began to make its mark. Ultimately, the Knob Hill became the greatest gold mine in the entire state and one of the

Horses pounding down dusty Clark Avenue on the Fourth of July, 1908, when Republic was the biggest and wildest town in the county.
(Photograph - Courtesy Provincial Archives of British Columbia)

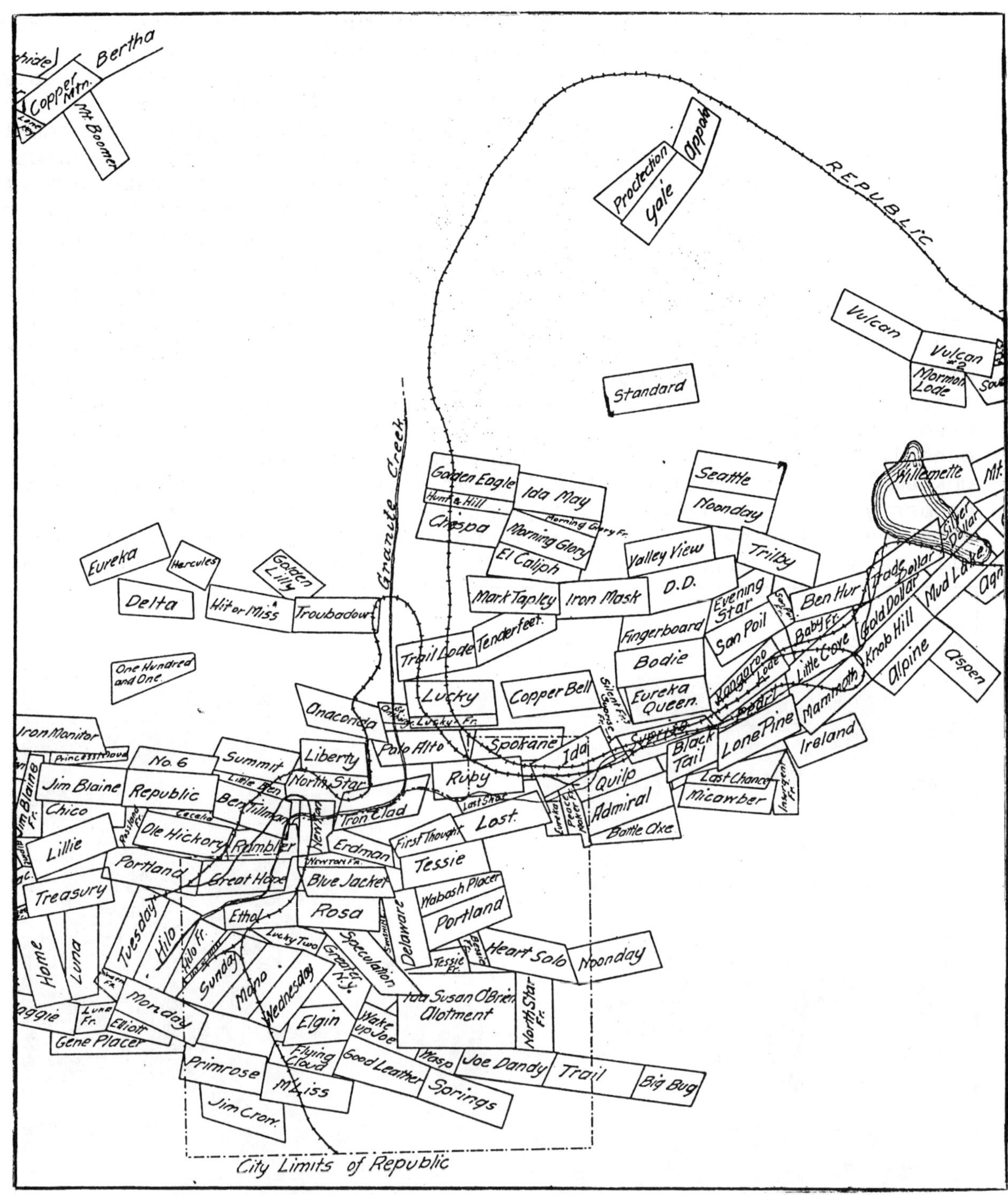

This map from Bulletin No. 1, Washington Geological Survey, shows the heart of Republic camp in 1910. The famous claims of the 1890s; Quilp, Republic, Insurgent, Jim Blaine, Lone Pine, Black Tail, Morning Glory, El Caliph, Surprise and many more are indicated on this map. The Knob Hill, ultimately to become the most illustrious gold mine in Republic history and one of the great gold producers of North America, had not yet come to the fore by that date. (Courtesy Dept. of Natural Resources)

most illustrious producers in the United States - yielding a staggering total of close to 2,400,000 troy ounces of gold during its lifetime, ensuring Republic's reputation as one of the greatest gold camps in the old west.

And those gold kings of yesterday, well known entrepreneurs like Patsy Clark and Frank Raberg; Clark, who made the right moves at the right times, went down in the annals of mining as one of the greatest mine-finders in the northwest. Raberg, once a millionaire mine owner and broker in Republic, doomed to die penniless and forgotten in 1911 in a little mining town called Manhattan, Nevada. Both once on an equal footing; the first the beneficiary of good fortune, the last the victim of the vageries of the mining world. Such was life in old Republic.

Today that historic town has changed. Clark Avenue certainly isn't as grand as it was, as many of its once imposing buildings are gone, the legacy of devastating fires over the last few decades. And those horses and riders don't come pounding down that avenue as they did on so many Fourth of July days so long ago when you might have run into characters like "White Dog" Burns, "Bum Mitt" Casey or "Big Foot" Allen in the Montana Saloon. But take a solitary walk up Eureka Gulch past those old workings or along Clark Avenue in the early morning - and some of the old glory floods back - that's Republic.

The "Hot Air" line; the old Spokane & British Columbia. Everyone helps out, including the passengers when the train is stuck.

(Photograph - Courtesy Provincial Archives of British Columbia)

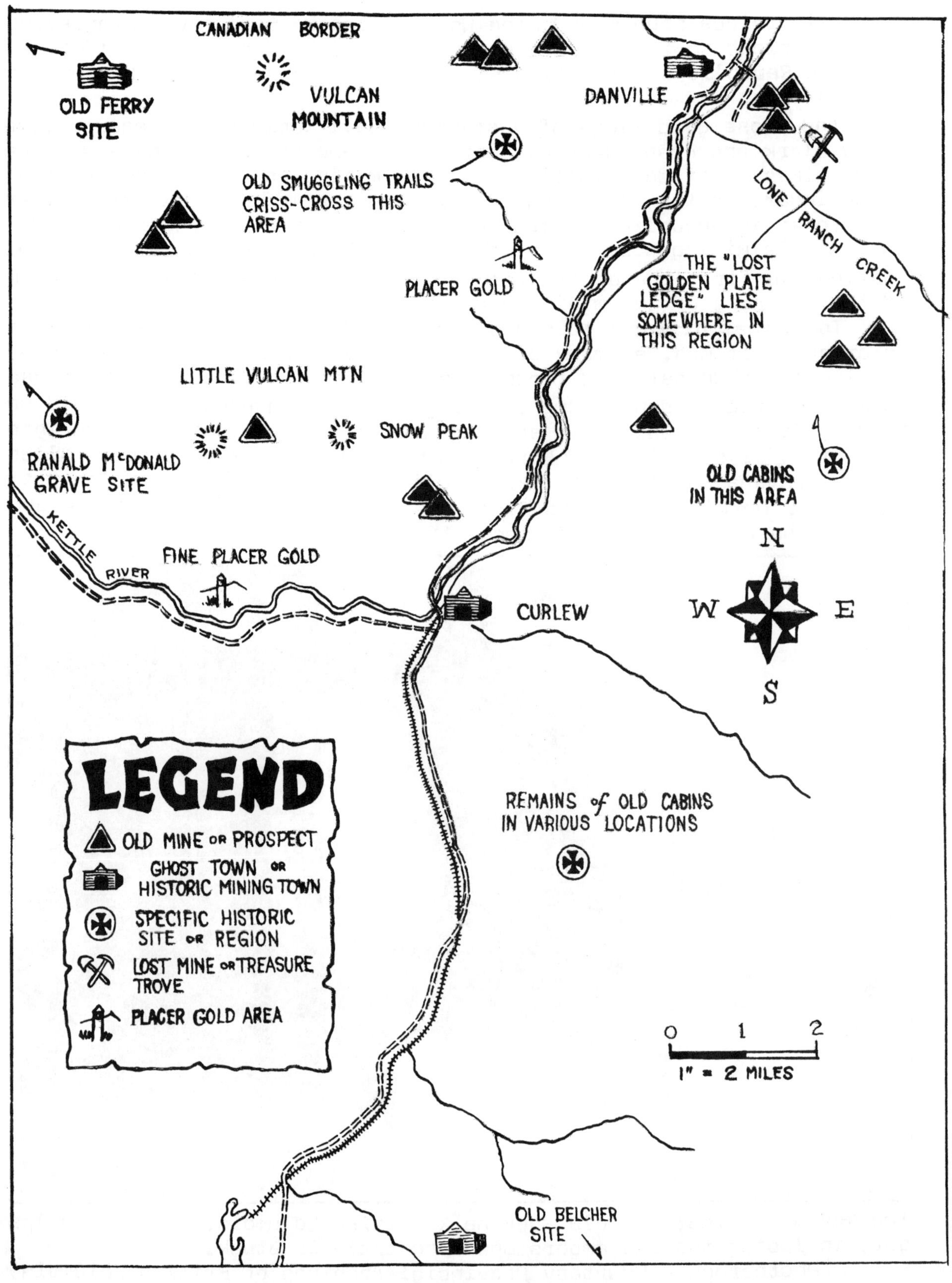

CANADIAN BORDER
OLD FERRY SITE
VULCAN MOUNTAIN
DANVILLE
OLD SMUGGLING TRAILS CRISS-CROSS THIS AREA
LONE RANCH CREEK
PLACER GOLD
THE "LOST GOLDEN PLATE LEDGE" LIES SOMEWHERE IN THIS REGION
LITTLE VULCAN MTN
SNOW PEAK
RANALD McDONALD GRAVE SITE
OLD CABINS IN THIS AREA
KETTLE RIVER
FINE PLACER GOLD
CURLEW
N
W
E
S
LEGEND
OLD MINE OR PROSPECT
GHOST TOWN OR HISTORIC MINING TOWN
SPECIFIC HISTORIC SITE OR REGION
LOST MINE OR TREASURE TROVE
PLACER GOLD AREA
REMAINS of OLD CABINS IN VARIOUS LOCATIONS
0 1 2
1" = 2 MILES
OLD BELCHER SITE

PLACER GOLD

Still yielding some fine placer gold on selected bars, the Kettle is also one of the most scenic and unspoiled rivers in the entire northwest and one of the most enjoyable to mine. Strawberry creek, Curlew creek and Big Goosmus creek have also produced placer gold in varying amounts, but the Kettle, although never a noted producer, continues to yield fine gold to those individuals who are satisfied with a meagre take from this splendid and memorable river.

Big Goosmus Creek ● This stream flows into the Kettle river south of Danville. It has produced some coarse gold although big boulders were a problem during mining. Most of the placer mining was undertaken in the 1920s and 1930s by local miners like Foley Payne and others. This creek may have yielded around 120 ounces.

Prospects: Unreliable ground. The paystreak is narrow and the water flow during dry seasons almost ceases.

This interesting photograph shows famous "Hellgate" on the Columbia. This was a dangerous passage on the river and one of many obstacles that the old time placer miners, and later the Chinese, were forced to run in their quest for gold.
(photograph - Courtesy: Eastern Washington State Historical Society)

Columbia River ● Once a fairly renowned and productive placer river. Since the various dams have raised the river's level, most of the old bars and benches which once yielded quantities of flour gold, are now under water. The early miners, and later the Chinese argonauts, worked places like Hellgate Bar, Rogers Bar, Turtle Rapids Bar, Ninemile Bar and scores of other places along the river for years.

Prospects: Only occasionally does high ground produce today. There was a day when the Columbia was worth mining in various locations in Ferry County, but they have long gone.

Fourth of July Creek ● This stream rises in Canada where it is known as July Creek. Although a small creek, several of its branches, like May creek and Skeff creek, were good producers of coarse gold. In the 1930s a local miner named Singer took out some gold on the lower part near Danville.

Prospects: Generally poor. Although the upper parts of this stream have yielded a number of nuggets and coarse gold, they are in Canada. The lower section of this creek, in Washington, is far poorer ground. An unlikely prospect.

One of a number of abandoned cabins and ranches in the Big Goosmus creek area near Danville. (Old Okanogan Publishing Company)

Granite Creek ● A much richer placer creek than is generally assumed. This little known gold stream rises to the west of Republic and flows eastward past that historic town before it finally joins the Sanpoil river. It has produced impressive quantities of placer gold since its discovery in 1896. The ground along this creek have been tightly held for many years by local placer miners. The gold was quite coarse with some nuggets, especially during the discovery years.

Prospects: Still some limited possibilities although Granite creek has been heavily hand mined in all its productive sections. The early reports state that "800 ounces" were recovered during the first season of mining. Evidently the shallow ground was quickly exhausted because Granite is generally considered almost mined out.

Other Prospects ● The Kettle River has produced some fine gold. The Kettle's gold was mostly produced from various bars by Chinese miners during the 1890s.

The famous "Long Alec" and his wife Mary standing by their log cabin.

TREASURES & LOST MINES

Danville, Washington - circa 1909. This photograph shows the town as it looked when mines like the Morning Star were yielding tons of gold rich ore and Danville was booming. (Courtesy Mrs. Helen Brinkman, Danville)

THE LOST GOLDEN PLATE LEDGE

Transfixed, the assayers stared at the sample. It was undoubtedly the richest ore specimen that they had ever laid eyes on, and they had seen many thousands of samples. It was a slab of rotten, reddish quartz nearly 18" long, about 10" wide and between 1" and 1½" thick. And it was laced through with "free gold;" so much of it that even assay office veterans were awestruck.

Eric S. Atwood, a young 21 year old assayer at the huge Granby Consolidated's Grand Forks smelter in that May of 1917, hefted the slab and was duly impressed by its extreme weight, something which he recalled in 1987, fully seventy years later.

The individual who had brought it into the smelter for refining was called John Falconer, a miner and sometimes prospector who came from Danville, a small mining town just on the United States side of the border, barely four miles south of the smelter which was located at Grand Forks, B.C. The strange story about its discovery, which he related to the employees at the Granby complex, was quite singular and equally astonishing.

The Granby smelter in Grand Forks in 1905. It was to this smelter that John Falconer took his amazing specimen of gold ore in 1917. For a variety of reasons the details of his find have remained lost until today.

He was working in Danville during the summer of 1912, he said, when a particularly violent electrical storm passed through the area. During this storm a lightning strike ignited a tree on a hillside to the south-east of the town. Noticing the fire, Falconer picked up a shovel, saddled up his horse, and set out for the blaze.

Crossing the Kettle river, he slowly began climbing toward the fire location. Part way, he stated, he came across a game trail and began following it. After some time on the trail it started to rain, but as he continued on toward the still burning tree, he recalled, his horse's hoof struck a flat slab of rock lying in the middle of the trail. He noticed, he said, that when the hoof hit the rock it gave off "an almost metallic ring." Proceeding along the trail for a short distance he finally came to a halt when he realized that the downpour had extinguished the fire. Turning around, he retraced his route and once again came across the rock slab lying on the trail. Idly curious, he dismounted and picked up the rock. As he lifted it, he related, he was astonished at its great weight.

He peered at the rock. It was criss-crossed with a brassy looking metal. "Pyrites," he thought, but intrigued by its weight, he decided to take it back with him. In the late afternoon he arrived back in

The Morning Star buildings, workings and waste dump can be seen in this photograph taken around 1910. It is quite plausible that John Falconer's Lost Golden Plate Ledge is a south-eastern extension of the Morning Star ore body. (Courtesy Mrs. Helen Brinkman, Danville)

Danville. Glad to be rid of his burden, he dropped the slab in his yard, walked into the house, and promptly forgot about it.

Some months passed, but one day when he came off shift from his job in the Virginia Mine, he saw the rock still lying where he had thrown it. Once again he picked it up - and this time he took a long look at it. It was unusual, most unusual, he decided, what he had assumed were pyrites originally, actually looked more like gold. He carried the specimen into his house and showed it to his wife, she, in turn, was equally intrigued. A rudimentary scratch test indicated, beyond a doubt, that the yellow metal was not pyrites, but was in fact, pure gold!

Falconer was sure that he could find the exact spot on the game trail where he had found the "float." He tried to retrace the route he had taken, he stated, but he was unable to locate it. His memory, he related sadly, had played him false. For five years he and his wife, day after day, relentlessly criss-crossed the area, searching for the game trail where he had found the ore. But there were scores of trails, he stated and they had been unable to find that original spot. They had, he went on to say, found a mineralized zone with a greenstone dyke, but they had never located the place where the rich piece of float had come from.

The hills surrounding Danville, especially to the east, are dotted with long abandoned mines like this one. It is generally assumed that the "Lost Ledge" is a buried extension of a mineralized zone in this area.

And that, Falconer concluded, was the story of the specimen he had brought in to be refined. At the conclusion of his narrative, the prospector broke off a small piece of the slab and presented it to the assayers. When interviewed in 1987, Eric Atwood stated that the piece measured approximately 2" by 2" and was placed on display in the mineral specimens case. The remainder of the ore slab, which weighed close to sixty pounds, was taken out to be refined.

A few days later the Granby Consolidated remitted a check for just over $1,000.00 to John Falconer. With gold at $20.67 a troy oz. in 1917, the specimen had yielded nearly fifty troy ounces, or just over four pounds of pure gold - almost unbelievable!

Shortly after, on Friday, June 1, 1917, a front page article in the GRAND FORKS GAZETTE added the following information:

MAY TURN DANVILLE RANCH INTO A MINE

Samples of ore heavily charged with gold have been exhibited by John Falconer as part of the ledge he discovered on the ranch near Danville owned by himself and a relative, former judge Logsdon.

"The vein, which is several inches in width, lies in a contact of decomposed quartz and greenstone," said Mr. Falconer. "Veins in kind are also found elsewhere in the decomposed mass, which appears to have a large area.

"In the greenstone dyke, which is 100 feet wide, I have opened three veins, three to eight feet wide, containing good values in copper and a little gold. I will trench the 100 foot body in search of other veins. At the point of great promise I will sink a shaft and drive a crosscut from the bottom of the shaft. The conditions appear to be highly favorable for the development of a copper-gold mine of large size.

"My wife and I have been prospecting in the neighborhood ever since our marriage five years ago when I found a little float. Every afternoon when I came off shift on the Virginia Mine we resumed the search. Our industry seems to have frightened some of the neighbors, one of whom proved up hurriedly as if to forstall the location of a gold mine on his ranch.

"The judge is not so enthusiastic over our discovery. The notoriety seems to have embarrassed him a little. He says it has forced him to put on a white shirt and collar on coming to Grand Forks."

A careful perusal of Falconer's later statement to the GAZETTE, however, reveals several discrepancies and omissions, both of which have an important bearing on the story. An analysis of the newspaper article is quite revealing.

Firstly, and probably intentionally, he neglected to disclose the details of the original discovery of the "float," which he had disclosed earlier to the Granby assayers. The specimen that Falconer brought in to be refined was spectacularly rich in gold, whereas in the article he stated that he had found three veins "containing good values in copper and a little gold." The greenstone dyke he found on his ranch was obviously a predominantly copper proposition, and not a staggeringly rich gold prospect. It appears that the ore specimen left at the smelter was the original piece of float and not from the prospect on his home ranch, indeed a yield of more than four pounds of pure gold from a single piece of float must be considered more than "a little gold." The statement, "My wife and I have been prospecting in the neighborhood ever since our marriage five years ago when I found a little float," is extremely important and indicative of the value that Falconer and his wife placed on that first piece of float. Rare indeed is the prospector who devotes half a decade in an attempt to find a copper prospect - but gold - now that's an entirely different proposition, especially when it was staggeringly

INCORPORATED UNDER THE LAWS OF WASHINGTON

№ 103 — 156 — SHARES

Morning Star Mining Company

FULLY PAID ... CAPITAL STOCK $100,000 — NON-ASSESSABLE

This Certifies ... Victor Nelson is the owner of ONE HUNDRED FIFTY-SIX (156) Shares of -----$1.00--------- each of the Capital Stock of Morning Star Mining Company transferable only on the books of the Corporation ... hereof in person or by Attorney upon surrender of ... properly endorsed.

In Witness Whereof, the said Corporation has caused this Certificate to be signed by its duly authorized officers and to be sealed with the Seal of the Corporation ... Spokane, Wash. this 24th day of January A.D. 1938

SECRETARY — PRESIDENT

SHARES $1.00 EACH

Stock certificate, Morning Star mine, Danville, 1938. A rare token from the Log Hotel and a quartz specimen with free gold in it are shown lying on the stock certificate. All three items are becoming relatively rare, especially the token which reads " Nelson, Wash."
(photograph - Courtesy Victor Nelson, Danville)

rich. Another indicator that Falconer did not prospect his own ranch initially is the phrase, "Our industry seems to have frightened some of the neighbors, one of whom proved up hurriedly as if to forstall the location of a gold mine on his ranch." Obviously, the Falconers were prospecting in other areas, but when they were unable to find the original ledge they came back and staked the copper prospect which was on their own ranch. Another key phrase is, "The judge is not so enthusiastic over our discovery...." Probably, as Judge Logsdon was a relative, he was in on the secret of the original discovery, hence his lack of enthusiasm over the staking of a copper prospect instead of the long anticipated gold ledge which Falconer had been searching for since 1912.

After examining the 1917 newspaper article in the GRAND FORKS GAZETTE and after interviewing E. S. Atwood and others, especially old timers from the Danville area, it seems that Falconer did indeed find a piece of incredibly rich float in 1912. After his five year, and unsuccessful, search failed to turn up the original ledge, he than staked the secondary copper prospect on his own property.

Today, somewhere in those rolling hills south-east of historic old Danville, beyond the river they call the Kettle, lies a ledge, prodigiously rich, and undoubtedly buried by overburden, which John Falconer searched for for so many years after his chance discovery in 1912 of a peculiar piece of incredibly rich ore, a flat slab of float so rich in gold that old timers referred to it as "the golden plate."

One fact is certain, the prospector who eventually finds that hidden ledge will be rewarded - beyond his wildest imagination.

The hills east of Danville, the source of the "Lost Ledge."

III
STEVENS COUNTY

INTRODUCTION

Stevens County - There are places in this county where history still casts its long shadows: Leadpoint and Marcus, Northport and Boundary. In those indelible places the mood of old lingers on.

And it's there in a myriad of other locations as well, it's on Windy Ridge and Gladstone Mountain where a roll call of mines with names like Lead Trust and Lead King, Red Iron and Wildcat, Keystone and Gladstone all hearken back to those years when mining was king.

Admittedly the Columbia is not the river it once was. Much of its old magic vanished forever when Grand Coulee tamed that majestic waterway more than half a century ago and inundated historic places like old Marcus, the original site of Fort Colville, the placer gold bars and ancient Indian encampments like Sxoie'lps and innumerable others.

But this is a land where other years are never far away. It is where the lone wolf can drift - beyond the main, along overgrown and long abandoned trails, back into the solitude of the mining country where the echoes of the 1890s are almost audible and the chances of discovering another million dollar mine like Electric Point cannot be dismissed. This is Stevens County.

A general store at historic Blue Creek, north of Chewelah. It, like nearby Addy, flourished briefly before fading.
(Photograph - Courtesy Stevens County Historical Society)

GHOST TOWNS

Four buildings still standing along once colorful Columbia Avenue in historic old Northport today. A booming smelter and mining town at the turn of the century, this interesting old border town, although hard hit by a series of devastating fires down through the years, still has that unusual atmosphere, an old mood which few towns retain.

and MINING TOWNS

ADDY

You might not know it's even there, but don't pass by old Addy. It's about seven miles northwest of Chewelah, just a few hundred yards west of Highway 395 - and it's been there for almost a century.

It was called Addy Station once and there was a time when it was a distribution center of some importance. Of course that was when the Spokane Falls & Northern made regular stops and mines like the Daisy, Silver Summit, Hanford, Nevada and half a dozen other mines close by were shipping hundreds of tons of rich silver ore, and the main beneficiary was Addy. The Deer Trail district, twenty-five miles southwest of the town, was also booming as was the nearby Chewelah district.

But eventually the mines played out and Addy, like so many other places dependent upon the longevity of the mines, also played out. It still has a number of buildings of historic significance on the west side of its main street and the surrounding district hearkens back to the turn of the century and better years. Daisy lies to the west, and Blue Creek just to the south - both as interesting in different ways as Addy. This is another area in Stevens County where the past seems to have stood still.

Addy - circa 1900, showing barely twenty buildings on the townsite. (photograph - Courtesy Eastern Washington State Historical Society)

An express office and store on the main street of Addy around 1911.
(photograph - Courtesy Stevens County Historical Society)

Derelict near Blue Creek and Addy.

Scenes from early day Addy. (Stevens County Historical Society)

BOSSBURG

"The stagecoach from Bossburg is in!

That was a common call during the late 1890s, not only in Stevens and Ferry counties, but also in those border towns in nearby British Columbia. In those years Bossburg was the great transportation center of Stevens County. Ideally located on the southern side of the Columbia River, it commanded routes to all of the four cardinal directions.

It came onto the scene with little fanfare but by 1901 it had a population of 600 and numerous freighting outfits who transported all types of mining supplies and machinery to mining towns in both of the counties and in British Columbia. It was so important that it claimed two telephone companies and a newspaper, The BOSSBURG JOURNAL, a town hall with a manager, two ferry companies, three saloons, three general stores and two hotels. And its busy main street was so wide that it could and did allow twelve horse outfits to make a full turn anywhere on the street.

But Bossburg lasted only as long as the mining boom. And when the mines close by; like the Young America, Silver Dollar, Uncle Sam, Gold Bug, Boston & Washington and several others shut down, the town wasn't far behind. Today a passerby would be hard pressed to realize that the town called Bossburg had ever even existed.

Early Bossburg. (Courtesy Eastern Washington State Historical Society)

A few remnants in old Bossburg. During the 1890s, this historic town was an important distribution point.

BOUNDARY

For a few hectic months it was a roaring and rollicking camp on the northern edge of the frontier. Located barely a stone's throw from the Canadian line, its single main street was lined with false-front buildings, the majority of them saloons.

At its height, in the 1890s, when the Spokane Falls and Northern Railroad was driving into the heart of the mineralized belt of British Columbia's rich West Kootenay District, the camp's population soared to almost 900. It was a typical railroad camp then, with all of the raw diversions of the day; sometimes deadly bare knuckle brawls, all night drinking, no limit poker games or other equally wide open games of chance, all designed to separate the construction men from their hard earned wages. But if the gamblers missed, the shadowy sandbaggers didn't. Many an unwary worker awoke in a ditch in the early hours of the morning with empty pockets and a lump on the head, a reminder of a late night sandbagging in rough old Boundary.

But the camp didn't last. When the railroad finally spanned the wild Pend Oreille with a bridge, the railroad workers quickly moved on, leaving the camp virtually deserted. For a few more years the town lingered on, struggling for its existence. In those declining years

Boundary, around 1899. It boomed and then quickly lapsed into a ghost camp. (photograph courtesy Stevens County Historical Society)

the Boundary Hotel, a post office and general store and a handful of people inhabited the site. Eventually, however, when "New Boundary," came into being south of the original townsite, the old town lapsed and finally vanished.

Today old time families like the Grahams and the Hartbauers no longer live in Boundary although those names are inextricably linked with its history. Passersby usually see only a barren and dusty flat but a much closer examination reveals the faint traces of that first camp - overgrown depressions where basements once stood and rows of rocks, unmoved in nearly a century, outlining old building sites, and to the west, between the little flat and the Columbia river, piles of tailings can still be seen, silent memorials to the placer miners of long ago. But that is all, there is little else to mark Boundary and those halcyon days of this once colorful camp.

The old camp of Boundary stands abandoned today although the basement depressions and barely discernible rows of rocks remain on the site, reminders of those years when Boundary was booming.

CEDARVILLE

There is only a handful of almost unknown mining ghost camps in Washington and one of these old towns was located in the little known Deer Trail District of southern Stevens County.

It was called Cedarville or Cedar Canyon during its high years, and it was, for a brief time, a rich and illustrious mining camp. In the early 1890s prospectors discovered deposits of high grade silver ore in a remote canyon deep in the mountains north-west of Spokane.

And what a discovery it was - with ore running steadily at over 200 ounces of silver per ton, it promised to become a leading silver producing district. And for a time it was just that. With mines like the famous Deer Trail, Legal Tender, Providence, Silver Seal, Silver Queen, Elephant, Cleveland and half a dozen other properties pouring out a steady stream of silver, a camp first called "Cedar Canyon" came into being. By 1897 it had a cluster of buildings including an hotel owned by the Smiths, Diamond's General Store, a livery stable, a log schoolhouse and no less than four saloons. By the time its population hit the 300 mark, Cedar Canyon had assumed the more grandiose name "Cedarville."

For close to eighteen years it was a small but bona fide mining town. Finally, when it became apparent that the richest silver mines were restricted to a small area near Cedar Canyon and that the values decreased at depth, the population began to decline. In 1911, when the rich Deer Trail, Providence and Legal Tender mines closed down, the die had been cast, and soon after Cedarville lay deserted.

An eerie silence now prevails where once the sounds of mining echoed through the valley - the Cedarville of old no longer exists.

This remarkable photograph shows "Cedar Canyon" in its early stages. (Courtesy Cheney Coles Museum, Eastern Washington Historical Society)

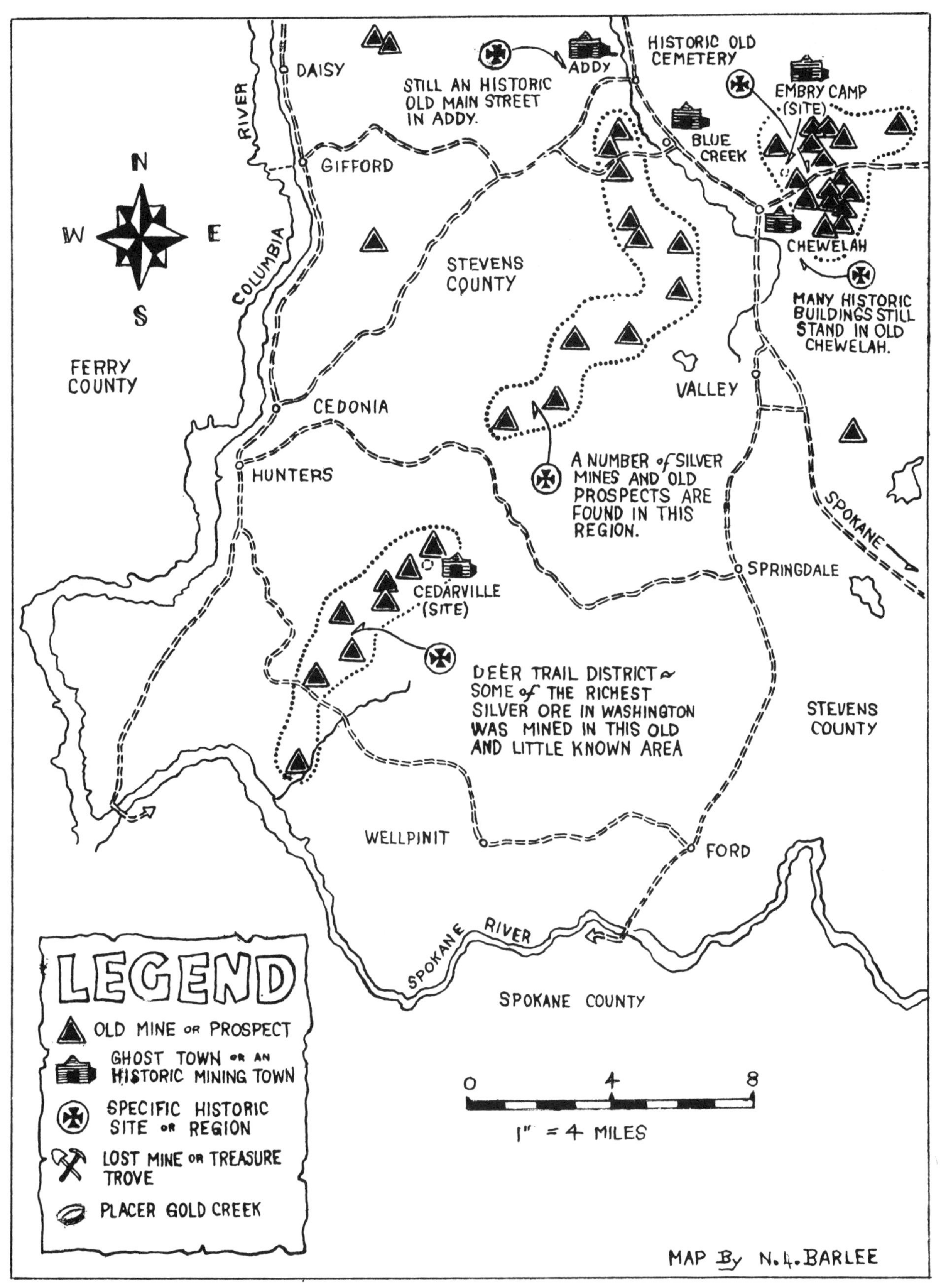
DAISY
ADDY
STILL AN HISTORIC OLD MAIN STREET IN ADDY.
HISTORIC OLD CEMETERY
EMBRY CAMP (SITE)
BLUE CREEK
GIFFORD
COLUMBIA RIVER
N
W
E
S
STEVENS COUNTY
CHEWELAH
MANY HISTORIC BUILDINGS STILL STAND IN OLD CHEWELAH.
FERRY COUNTY
VALLEY
CEDONIA
HUNTERS
A NUMBER of SILVER MINES AND OLD PROSPECTS ARE FOUND IN THIS REGION.
SPOKANE
SPRINGDALE
CEDARVILLE (SITE)
DEER TRAIL DISTRICT ~ SOME of THE RICHEST SILVER ORE IN WASHINGTON WAS MINED IN THIS OLD AND LITTLE KNOWN AREA
STEVENS COUNTY
WELLPINIT
FORD
SPOKANE RIVER
SPOKANE COUNTY
LEGEND
OLD MINE OR PROSPECT
GHOST TOWN OR AN HISTORIC MINING TOWN
SPECIFIC HISTORIC SITE OR REGION
LOST MINE OR TREASURE TROVE
PLACER GOLD CREEK
0
4
8
1" = 4 MILES
MAP By N.L.BARLEE

CHEWELAH

Venture out beyond Chewelah, in almost any direction, and history waits. It's a misleading place. You'd never guess that it was a mining town once, but it's steeped in mining history.

It started during the 1880s, after the Old Dominion mine had been discovered east of nearby Colville. The bullion flowing from it started a stampede of prospectors who flooded into the region. In 1883, silver and lead deposits were discovered at Embry Camp, barely a mile east of Chewelah. Soon a series of other strikes were made on Jay Gould Ridge, Eagle Mountain and Quartzite Mountain. Soon, properties like Keystone, Chewelah Silver, Copper King, Jay Gould, Chinto, Eagle, Mullan, Amazon and almost twenty other mines and prospects. Embry Camp soon vanished and Chewelah came into its own. With ore wagons laden with silver and copper ore and a railroad running through the town, business activity increased steadily. By 1910, Chewelah had a population of nearly 1,500 and a wide main street flanked by impressive buildings. Unlike a great many other mining towns in the county, the mines around Chewelah kept producing, well into the 1950s.

Today those great mines like United Copper are closed and silent, but Chewelah, with its old fashioned look and colorful history is still there, a unique reminder of the durability of an old mining town.

A turn of the century photograph of a mine south-west of Chewelah.
(photograph - Courtesy Stevens County Historical Society)

Main Street in Chewelah, probably somewhere around 1915. This historic town, unlike most mining towns, weathered good times and bad and was little changed. (Courtesy Eastern Washington State Historical Society)

The picturesque Chewelah cemetery east of town.

LEADPOINT

"Dollars were made round to go around - and I sure make them go around!" It was a grandiose announcement but it was close to the mark and the individual who made that statement was one of the most colorful men ever to set foot in Leadpoint.

He went by the unlikely name of Joshua Yoder and he was a man of great contrasts. He was a huge man, standing well over six feet and weighing over 200 pounds. Illiterate, with a hair-trigger temper and a loud, booming voice coupled with an overbearing manner, he was a most impressive figure; feared by many, respected by all.

Despite his obvious flaws, he had some qualities which balanced the scales; he was doggedly loyal to his friends and generous to a fault. And his word was legendary, once given - never broken.

Leadpoint is a little known mining camp located in the mountains southeast of Northport. Established during the early 1890s when high-grade deposits of lead were found in the hills close by, it became the main distribution point for the many mines in the area. But with the exception of the Gladstone and several others, most of the mines were small shippers and Leadpoint remained an insignificant camp.

Boarding house still standing in Leadpoint today, one of many historic places in this little known mining camp.

It came into its own in 1915 when a trapper named Chris Johnson decided to investigate a spot where lightning always struck. He hiked into the area and after wandering around he eventually located a tree blackened and split, obviously by numerous lightning strikes. Curious, he walked towards it and then noticed several pieces of galena lying on the ground. He casually picked them up and placed them in his pack. He then returned to Leadpoint where he set them on the windowsill in his cabin.

Several months later Joshua Yoder happened by, dropped in on the trapper, and noticed the galena ore on the sill. He picked them up and examined them. Yoder was the complete prospector and quickly saw that it was high grade lead. Excited, he asked Johnson where he had found the ore. The trapper waved his hand vaguely toward the western hills. Yoder quickly offered the trapper a deal; if Johnson would lead him to the location, he would locate it, give Johnson a third interest, keep a third interest himself and give a third interest to his grubstaker, a high-rolling character named Art Young.

Later that morning the two men set out. By noon, after wandering aimlessly for several hours, they decided to have a quick lunch before resuming the search. They sat down on a handy log and started eating. At that juncture a cheeky red pine squirrel started chattering. Yoder

The mine buildings at the renowned Gladstone mine on Windy Ridge. The region on all sides of Leadpoint was mining country.

picked up a rock to throw at it, then noticed that the rock was heavy, very heavy. He examined it - it was a piece of high grade lead. Yoder jumped up, gesticulating wildly. A moment later he picked up another piece of ore, then another and another. They had found an incredibly rich chimney of galena. Nearby they found the lightning scarred tree. On July 2, 1915, Joshua Yoder recorded the claim which they named the Electric Point because of its unusual tendancy to attract lightning.

The Electric Point ultimately became one of the most illustrious mines in Stevens County, producing millions of dollars in profits for its owners. Chris Johnson soon sold his interest to a consortium from Spokane for $22,000.00, which he eventually frittered away. Art Young retained his interest and lived high off the hog; sometimes impressing the local prospectors by starting his campfire with a handful of bills. But Young came to a sad end; dying after a heavy drinking bout on his way to Alaska. Joshua Yoder, who "lived like a prince" for many years after, cut a wide swath in northern Stevens County, especially after his marriage to a much younger local beauty. But he too was to suffer. His wife died soon after their marriage and the broken-hearted miner, to commemorate her, spent $5,000.00 on a stone crypt. Later Yoder was murdered on his ranch at Deep Lake by a crazed hired hand by the name of Bigler. Thus the three original owners of the famed Electric Point

Stagecoaches from the Hotel Colville in front of the Columbia stables in nearby Colville - circa 1907.

(photograph - Courtesy Stevens County Historical Society)

mine failed to benefit to any lasting degree from the massive lode of almost pure lead which extended and widened to a depth of 900 feet.

Mainly on the strength of the Electric Point, Leadpoint grew to a respectable population of nearly 200. It had an hotel, a big general store, a barber shop and several other businesses.

Now Leadpoint is there in name only; half a dozen old, abandoned buildings remain standing on or near the townsite, but the school bell that tolled for so many years no longer rings and the once busy mines are closed.

But it is the kind of region that continues to draw prospectors, wanderers who know that there are other rich chimneys of ore, hidden under overburden in the hills nearby. So they fan out, searching for float or other signs of mineralization, looking for another deposit as rich as the Electric Point.

You won't be disappointed with historic Leadpoint. It has it all; dozens of abandoned mines, deserted buildings scattered throughout the region, historic trails, picturesque old cemeteries and lost mines.

Joshua Yoder's last resting place in the Deep Creek Cemetery which is between Northport and Leadpoint. Murdered by a man he had befriended, Yoder lies buried in this expensive crypt.

MARCUS

I remember it well, but that was almost half a century ago. It had that certain charm, some towns do - Marcus did.

It was ideally situated to command the traffic of the river, and that river, the Columbia, was the highway of the old West once. Every trader, trapper and prospector heading into that upper Columbia region passed by Marcus.

It wasn't always called "Marcus." When the fur traders ruled the Northwest it was known as "Old Fort." Later it came to be called, at least for a few years, "White's Landing." But when a prominent trader named Marcus Oppenheimer opened up a general store that dominated the town and prospered mightily, the town gradually assumed a new name, it became "Marcus," and the name stuck. Oppenheimer, knowing a good thing when he saw it, stayed put. When he arrived in 1863 he realized that the site was strategically located and that Marcus would eventually benefit. But it was a long wait for Oppenheimer, it was 1885 before it was given post office status, when its population was hovering at the 50 mark.

But the town slowly began to live up to its expectations. By 1910 its population had climbed tn a respectable 300; its busy main street

Marcus around 1900. It was quite a town in those days. A. C. Wetterer was the big merchant. (Courtesy - Stevens County Historical Society)

Stores on the main street of Marcus during the prosperous years – circa 1908. (photo courtesy – Eastern Washington State Historical Society)

The site of historic Marcus begins to vanish under the rising waters in 1940. (photo courtesy – Eastern Washington State Historical Society)

and business section reflected the general prosperity which northern Stevens County was enjoying during those years. The Spokane Falls and Northern Railroad proved to be a solid economic anchor and the silver and gold mines on both sides of the Columbia were producing hundreds of thousands of dollars worth of precious metals every year, and this activity, coupled with renewed confidence after nearly a full decade of prosperity, consolidated the position of Marcus.

Unfortunately those halcyon years eventually waned as the silver and gold properties, one by one, began to close their operations. The impact was imperceptible at first, but gradually even long established merchants, including those of the tight knit German speaking business community, with names like Wetterer, Schulze, Zwang and Wurzburg, began to feel the pinch and cut back. And the gloom intensified when the once great Northport smelter finally closed and was dismantled.

So Marcus, like most of those little towns in the upper part of the county edged into the depression years. But the greatest blow was yet to come; an announcement that was to doom Marcus and the very site upon which it stood - Marcus would be flooded by the rising waters of a new lake created after the completion of Grand Coulee Dam. Finally, in 1940, the inevitable happened - Marcus vanished beneath the waters.

Today there is a new Marcus, high on a bench above the original townsite. It's a picturesque little town, but it isn't quite the same as that first Marcus, that colorful town of half a century ago.

Several buildings from old Marcus on the 'new' site on the bench above the site of old Marcus.

NORTHPORT

The river still flows just beyond Columbia Avenue, as it has for countless years, but that avenue, once so boisterous and colorful, is not the thoroughfare it was in those turbulent days when Northport was still young. Down through the years this old town has been ravaged by a series of devastating fires and staggered by closures - any one of which would have doomed a lesser town, but somehow it survived, and despite those setbacks, there is still much about this historic town that hearkens back to the Northport of old.

Northport, like many old towns in the northern part of the state, was founded on the uncertain fortunes of mining. In 1890, on a flank of Red Mountain in British Columbia, north of the Columbia and barely across the boundary line, Joe Bourgeois and Joe Moris, two prospectors of French-Canadian origin, made a series of electrifying discoveries. These strikes were of such magnitude that the mining world was set on its ear. The mining men of Spokane were quickly off the mark and soon secured the bonanza properties; the Le Roi, War Eagle and Centre Star mines for themselves. Daniel Chase Corbin, the railroad tycoon of the

The original Silver Crown hotel in Northport around 1898. In that era Northport had such amenities as an opera house, a railroad, a bank and a population pushing 2,000. (photograph - courtesy Jack Murphy)

The last surviving smokestack at the original smelter. It is one of the last remaining in the state.

Some tokens and a few coins found in Northport. In the early 1960s, more than 600 coins and tokens were found by one individual under a section of the old boardwalk. Surprisingly, one section of boardwalk, buried by a foot and a half of overburden, still remained intact in 1988.

Inland Empire quickly sized up the situation. By 1892 his construction gangs were hard at work, rapidly laying track along the south side of the Columbia river, heading for a barren flat close to the border with Canada. The first train of the Spokane Falls & Northern chugged into the camp on the flat in 1892. It was called Northport and its one real asset was a newspaperman named Billy Hughes. Hughes, a great booster, was already publishing the NORTHPORT NEWS. By the following year, the camp had become a town, with a real hotel, a dancehall, two saloons, a mercantile store and more people pouring in almost hourly; including more than a few elegant ladies of leisure. In early 1893 a fire swept through the business district, leaving it in ruins. It was the first of the great Northport fires and the first of a series of disasters to plague the town.

But the setback was only temporary. By 1896 Northport was really coming into its own. The north half of the Colville Indian Reservation had been opened up and hundreds of prospectors and miners used Northport as their jumping off spot. Buildings were going up everywhere as everyone got in on the action. In nearby Rossland the illustrious gold mines were gaining a worldwide reputation for their richness. By 1898 the LeRoi smelter, a huge complex to refine the ore from the renowned LeRoi mine, was being constructed, a railroad bridge had been thrown

Columbia Avenue in Northport in the early days. Northport anticipated that it would become the county seat then. Alas, that honor was given to nearby Colville. (Courtesy - Stevens County Historical Society)

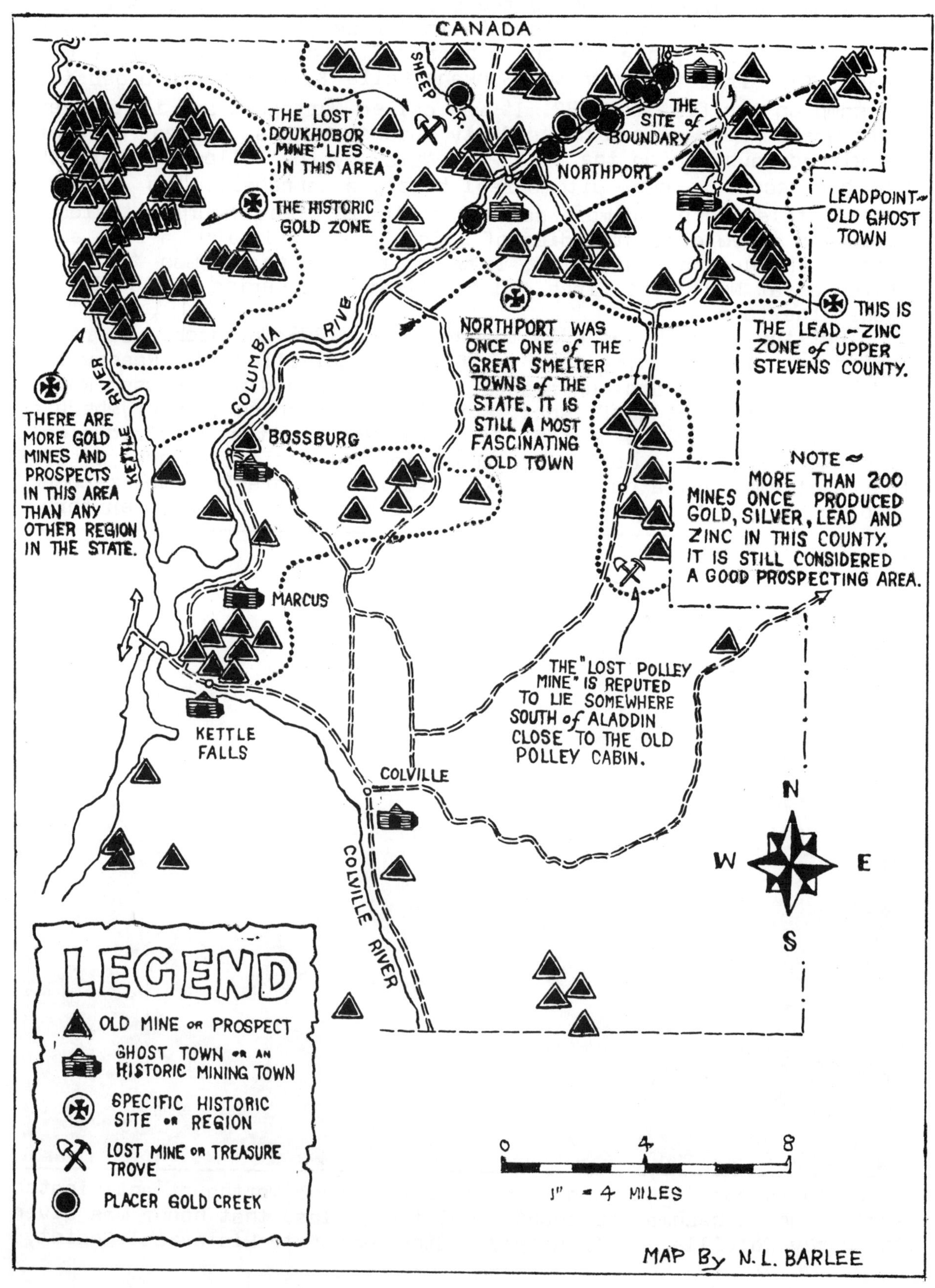
CANADA
SHEEP CR.
THE "LOST DOUKHOBOR MINE" LIES IN THIS AREA
THE HISTORIC GOLD ZONE
THE SITE of BOUNDARY
NORTHPORT
LEADPOINT ~ OLD GHOST TOWN
THIS IS THE LEAD-ZINC ZONE of UPPER STEVENS COUNTY.
NORTHPORT WAS ONCE ONE of THE GREAT SMELTER TOWNS of THE STATE. IT IS STILL A MOST FASCINATING OLD TOWN
COLUMBIA RIVER
KETTLE RIVER
THERE ARE MORE GOLD MINES AND PROSPECTS IN THIS AREA THAN ANY OTHER REGION IN THE STATE.
BOSSBURG
NOTE ~ MORE THAN 200 MINES ONCE PRODUCED GOLD, SILVER, LEAD AND ZINC IN THIS COUNTY. IT IS STILL CONSIDERED A GOOD PROSPECTING AREA.
MARCUS
THE "LOST POLLEY MINE" IS REPUTED TO LIE SOMEWHERE SOUTH of ALADDIN CLOSE TO THE OLD POLLEY CABIN.
KETTLE FALLS
COLVILLE
COLVILLE RIVER
N
W
E
S
LEGEND
OLD MINE OR PROSPECT
GHOST TOWN OR AN HISTORIC MINING TOWN
SPECIFIC HISTORIC SITE OR REGION
LOST MINE OR TREASURE TROVE
PLACER GOLD CREEK
0
4
8
1" = 4 MILES
MAP By N.L. BARLEE

The Northport smelter, probably taken prior to 1905. This huge smelting works was the major reason why the town became so important for almost two decades.
(photograph - Courtesy Archives of British Columbia)

The Northport smelter - circa 1899. The fortunes of Northport depended on this great smelting works. When it closed down Northport declined.

Looking down Second Street toward Columbia Avenue around 1915. The best years had passed by then, and although its population had slipped, many of its citizens hung on, hoping vainly for a revival.
(Photograph courtesy Kuk's Tavern, Northport)

across the Columbia and the railroad had reached Rossland, the famous "Golden City" of the Canadian west and the ore began to flow into the Northport smelter. Although another serious fire destroyed almost all of three blocks in the business area, the town barely faltered. By the end of the year Northport's population was approaching the 2,000 mark and some of its more substantial citizens were entertaining ideas of becoming the county seat. It was an imposing place then, with all of the glitter, noise and action that only a boom town has.

Those days, however, were coming to an end. The LeRoi management passed into English hands and the smelter, with much of its custom ore now being refined on the Canadian side, began to slip. The population, for the first time, also declined. The State Bank, once so prosperous, noticed that some local businesses were running into difficulties and others had closed their doors.

The smelter, the economic mainstay, hampered by lack of ore and by strikes, limped along. Finally, in the early morning of July 29, 1914, the greatest of all of the Northport fires levelled almost all of the downtown business district. It was the final catastrophe for the town.

Northport never really recovered from that date onward. This time the businesses weren't rebuilt as they had been in 1893 and in 1898. A pall settled uneasily over the town and deepened when the smelter finally closed down and was dismantled. By the 1930s even the most optimistic realized that the glory days of Northport had gone forever.

Deadman's Eddy hasn't changed much and there is still a mood in this town which recalls the memories of the glory times. Many people linger in this historic town and you'll understand why if you walk down Columbia Avenue sometime.

A few items from early Northport in the Dennis Brooks Collection.

PLACER GOLD

Some tailings along the Columbia river, just downriver from the old camp of Boundary. For decades Chinese miners toiled along this section of the Columbia, patiently mining the bench gravels for gold. Somewhere close by lie three overgrown and long forgotten graves, the last resting place of a trio of unknown Oriental argonauts who mined close to these diggings in another century. Even today, from China Bend to Northport and beyond to the border, there are innumerable signs of placer mining activity.

Columbia River ● This magnificent river still yields some placer gold to the occasional panner. Most of the gold is fine and is found from Northport to the Canadian line. The Chinese worked this stretch of the river for decades and recovered significant quantities of flour gold. The majority of the placer mining was on the south side of the river, mainly west of old Boundary. There are, however, places on the north side of the river which have been heavily mined.

Prospects: Not good although there are numerous places where small quantities of fine gold can be panned.

Big Sheep Creek ● This creek is also known as Sheep Creek and is a a northern tributary of the Columbia and enters that river east of old Northport. It was mined, mainly by Chinese, prior to 1890 and was, if reports are to be believed, relatively rich south of the canyon. Some coarse gold was recovered and this stream was mined fairly heavily in several sections.

Prospects: Not spectacular. There is still some occasional but not too productive mining going on from time to time. An interesting creek but don't count on it to produce much today.

The great Northport fire of 1914 which destroyed most of the business district; a blow from which Northport never really recovered.
(Photograph - Courtesy Stevens County Historical Society)

TREASURES & LOST MINES

A deserted homestead close by the road up to Gold Creek and the little known "Lost Doukhobor Mine" region. A well kept local secret for nearly six decades, some local prospectors have spent years looking for it.

THE LOST DOUKHOBOR LEDGE

Conservative, deliberate and cautious, he was certainly not the type of man who habitually chased after rainbows. And yet summer after summer, year after year, Roy Clark made an annual journey, a secretive and well planned trip into a little known triangle across the river from historic Northport, to an area close to the Canadian border in northern Stevens County.

Clark was searching for a mine which had been discovered in 1929, a find known locally by the old timers as "The Lost Doukhobor Ledge." Roy Clark, like so many others before and since, was unsuccessful in his long quest although he and a select handful of Northport pioneers, were convinced that it did, in fact, exist.

And their certainty was well founded and based upon more than just vague rumor. It was well documented and there were witnesses who were there at the time of discovery and saw the spectacular ore.

In the fall of 1929, after a particularly dry summer, a lightning strike started a small blaze in the Gold creek basin. Gold creek is a minor stream that flows into Sheep creek, a tributary of the Columbia. The area is north of Flagstaff Mountain and just beyond Hubbard Ridge.

Sheep creek. The search for the "Lost Doukhobor Ledge" began here. The mine seekers followed this stream and then turned west on Gold creek.

The fire, although initially small, rapidly began to spread. The Ranger in charge, M. R. "Buck" Hankins, hoping to contain the blaze, quickly sent in a four man firefighting crew, anticipating that they might be able to put it out before it spread any farther. Unknown to Hankins, however, his Canadian counterpart, stationed only a few miles away, in Rossland, B. C., receiving reports that the fire was starting to run out of control, sent a supression crew of twenty-five into the fire site. Most of the Canadians were Doukhobors; a religious sect in the West Kootenay region, and many were experienced fire fighters. By the time they arrived on the scene, however, the fire was crowning and out of control. The twenty-nine men headed into the Gold creek basin, hoping to throw up a fireguard to prevent it from spreading farther to the east. By nightfall, after working frantically, they finally managed to put in a narrow guard. But it was too narrow, barely half an hour later the now raging inferno jumped the guard and swept into the camp. The men scattered, running for their lives before the fire. Finally, safely out of reach, they rendezvoued and counted - twenty-seven men. Two of their crew were missing! A roll call revealed that the missing men were two Doukhobors from Rossland, both with years of experience in fire control. But their compatriots were worried and they had good reasons to be worried, the fire had been crowning when they fled from

Kuk's Tavern in Northport

their first camp, with the trees literally exploding on either side of them as they ran. Other firefighters had been burned to death in similar conditions and they assumed the worst for their two comrades. But, considering the hazardous conditions, they had no choice, they would have to wait until the first light of morning before they sent out a search party.

At dawn, just as the search party was preparing to leave, the two missing Doukhobors suddenly appeared. At the same time a young man named Ray Wiley came into camp from the opposite direction. He had been sent in by Hankins with water for the crew. Although Wiley was still a teenager, he was surprised to find that the camp was in an uproar. Informed that two men had returned after going missing, he naturally assumed that the other Doukhobors were elated with their almost miraculous deliverance from the all consuming fire. Then he noticed that the Doukhobors remained in a tight knot and were passing something from hand to hand, accompanied by much excited babbling in Ukrainian, their native language. Edging closer to the group, he saw that there were two objects being passed around and examined by the assembled men. The objects were pieces of ore, obviously galena. Almost six decades later Wiley remembered with clarity that "It was fine grained argentite - high grade silver ore." It was spectacular

The brick "Mammoth Building" still stands in Northport. Many other turn of the century structures also grace this historic old town.

looking ore and elicited gasps of admiration from the firefighters, most of whom had at least a passing knowledge of geology.

The two Doukhobors then related an astonishing story. They had become separated from the main group during the confusion the night before and had fled wildly before the fire, barely keeping ahead of the flames. Finally they managed to get far enough ahead to look for refuge. Just as they were approaching exhaustion, they spotted a rock slide. Realizing that it was probably the safest place around, they decided to stay overnight in the rocks near its base; well out of the timber - aware that rocks don't catch fire but timber does. And they stayed put all night sleeping fitfully and uncomfortably while the fire, roaring and crackling, swept on by them. At first light, they arose, gathered up their tools, and prepared to move out.

But as they picked their way slowly through the slide, working towards its base, they stumbled across a vein of galena. They paused to examine it. It was galena alright and it looked like it was high grade galena. Using their axe as a hammer, they managed to break off two pieces from the ledge and decided to take the samples with them for eventual assay.

The others stared at the samples, turning them over and over in their hands as they looked at them. Ray Wiley remembered that they

An abandoned miners' cabin close by Big Sheep creek. It was in this area where the two Doukhobors discovered the rich silver ledge.

were only about five inches by six inches and weighed perhaps seven pounds each. Finally, after the specimens had been passed around the circle of men several times, the discoverers retrieved them and put them into their packs, stating that they would have an assay run at the C. M. & S. Co. assay office in Trail, B. C., as soon as they got back, to see if the ore was as valuable as it appeared to be.

Many days later, with the forest fire under control at last, the Doukhobors returned to Rossland. Several months elapsed but finally, in the late spring of 1930, the two Doukhobors returned to Northport accompanied by a pair of geologists.

The ore samples, it turned out, had assayed at over 1,000 ounces of silver a ton - bonanza ore! Confident that they could easily locate the rock slide and the rich ledge of galena, the ecstatic discoverers, accompanied by the geologists, headed north - into the valley of Big Sheep creek. Late in the afternoon they wheeled west, into the Gold creek basin.

But it was a far different Gold creek valley than it had been a summer before. The forest fire had devastated the basin. Charred and blackened stumps, burned deadfalls and a desolate valley greeted the prospectors.

Undaunted, the two Doukhobors, still convinced that they could find the rock slide, picked their way through the burn. And all that afternoon and the next day, and the day after that, they crossed and recrossed the basin, working carefully as they proceeded west up the little valley, looking vainly for the slide. They found some slides, some big, some small, but none of them proved to be the right one.

Finally their food ran out and they were forced to give up the search. Deeply disappointed, they returned to Northport, swearing to come back again to resume the search. And they did return, making four more trips into the Gold creek area, but each time they returned empty handed.

Eventually, the two Doukhobors gave up, but the search was taken up by other prospectors, men who were familiar with the details or who had actually seen the ore, and remained convinced that the ledge was somewhere in or near the Gold creek basin. So the search continued, through the thirties and on into the forties. But none of these men, many of them dedicated prospectors, ever found the rock slide where the two Doukhobors had discovered the galena ledge. They did find rock slides in the basin of Gold creek, but none of them was the right one, not one had a band of high grade silver ore. And finally they too gave up the quest.

But this is one of those rare and fascinating lost mine stories where the facts are difficult to dismiss. Of that initial supression crew of twenty-nine, three of them are still living and each recalls the details of that day in 1929 with absolute clarity. They remember the two missing men coming back to camp with the high grade ore and the excitement the samples generated after they were passed around.

It was one of those rare and indelible moments which the mind's eye captures and retains, often for a lifetime.

The facts are clear. The 1929 forest fire in the basin of Gold creek is well documented and remembered. Ray Wiley, who carried the water into the crew during that fire, still lives on the north side of the Columbia on his ranch at Rattlesnake creek, just south of the Gold creek basin. Wiley, like so many other old timers in the region, is convinced that the ledge is there - he was there and he saw the ore. Over the decades, Wiley, a well known prospector, has made a number of trips into the basin in search of the lost ledge, but he, like Roy Clark and the others, failed to locate that rich deposit of silver.

So in that Gold creek region north of historic Northport, lies a rock slide, and somewhere under that slide is the ledge of galena, with ore so rich that it averages over 1,000 ounces of silver in each ton. Recent slides of rock may have covered that fabulous ledge - but it's there. And one day someone will find it, and that person will be fortunate indeed because the mysterious "Lost Doukhobor Ledge" has long been one of the closely guarded secrets of Stevens County.

A parade in Northport - circa 1898. Quite a float for those years. But Northport was the fastest growing town in Stevens County then.
(photograph - Courtesy Jack Murphy, Northport)

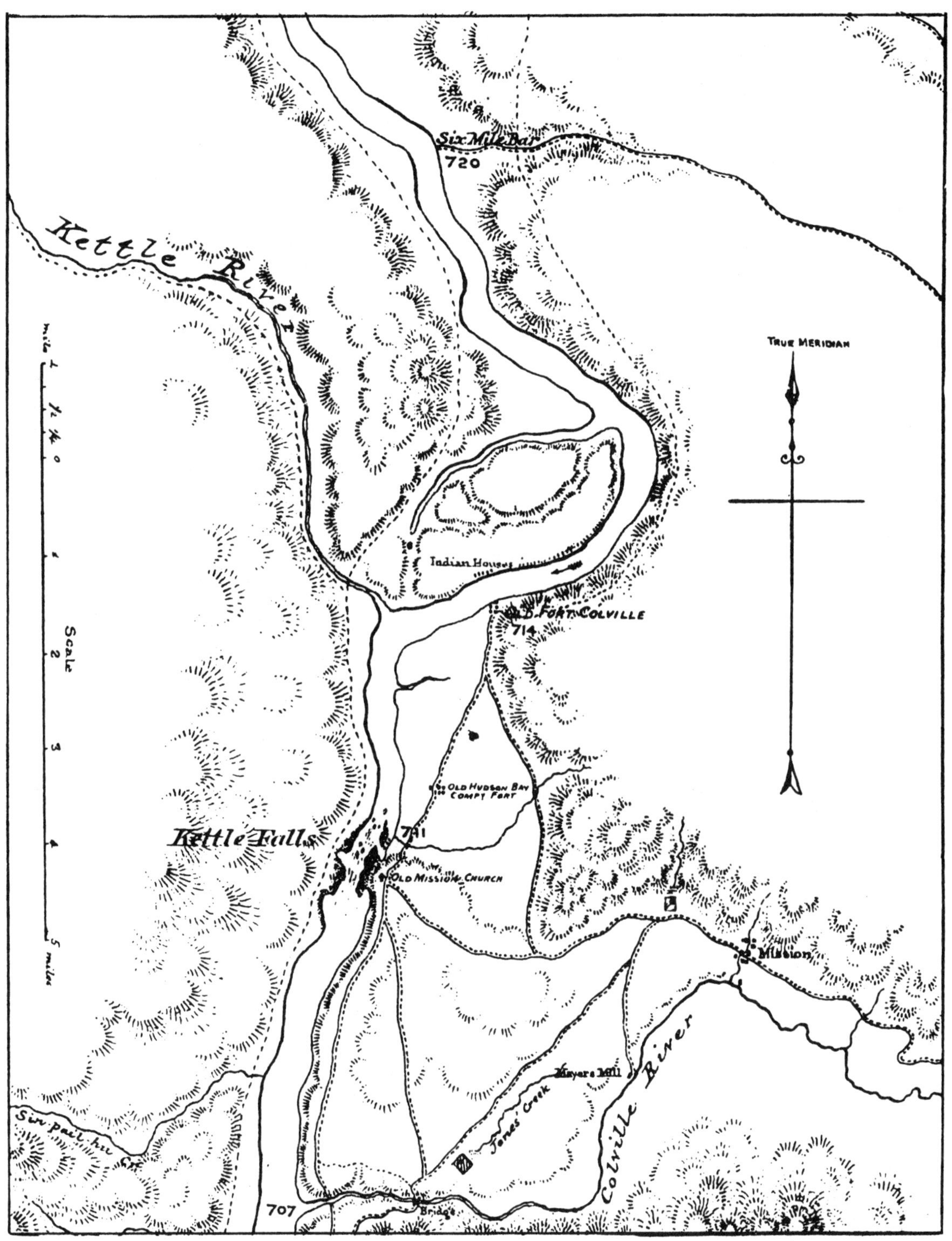

Detail of one of the map sheets from Lt. T. W. Symons 1881 Report on the Upper Columbia River and the Great Plain of the Columbia. This sheet shows old Kettle Falls and the original Fort Colville.

JANNI'S CHIMNEY OF ORE

He was a colorful and talented man who played many roles during his varigated career. His name was Peter Janni and he was born in 1874 in Grimaldi, Italy. As a boy he followed his father into the railroad camps of the far west. At a young age he was hired on by the Northern Pacific Railroad and worked his way across the northern plains into Montana, Idaho and finally into Washington. As a day laborer receiving $2.00 a day for a backbreaking ten hours, he quickly became adept with a pick and shovel, a sledge hammer and a wheelbarrow.

From time to time he also tried his hand at mining and gained some valuable knowledge, information which ultimately served him well. In 1893 he arrived in Northport as part of a construction gang laying track into Canada. He returned to Northport in 1902 to work at the smelter. Janni, a quick study with an engaging personality, was always looking around for new opportunities and booming Northport had many of them. Soon he was serving as an interpreter and Acting Inspector for the U. S. Immigration Service but since boyhood limestone quarries had been a source of continuing fascination for him. Finally, early in 1923, he purchased a magnificent limestone quarry south of Northport. For many years Janni shipped thousands of tons of fine limestone to points all through Washington, but there was more than limestone in Peter Janni's

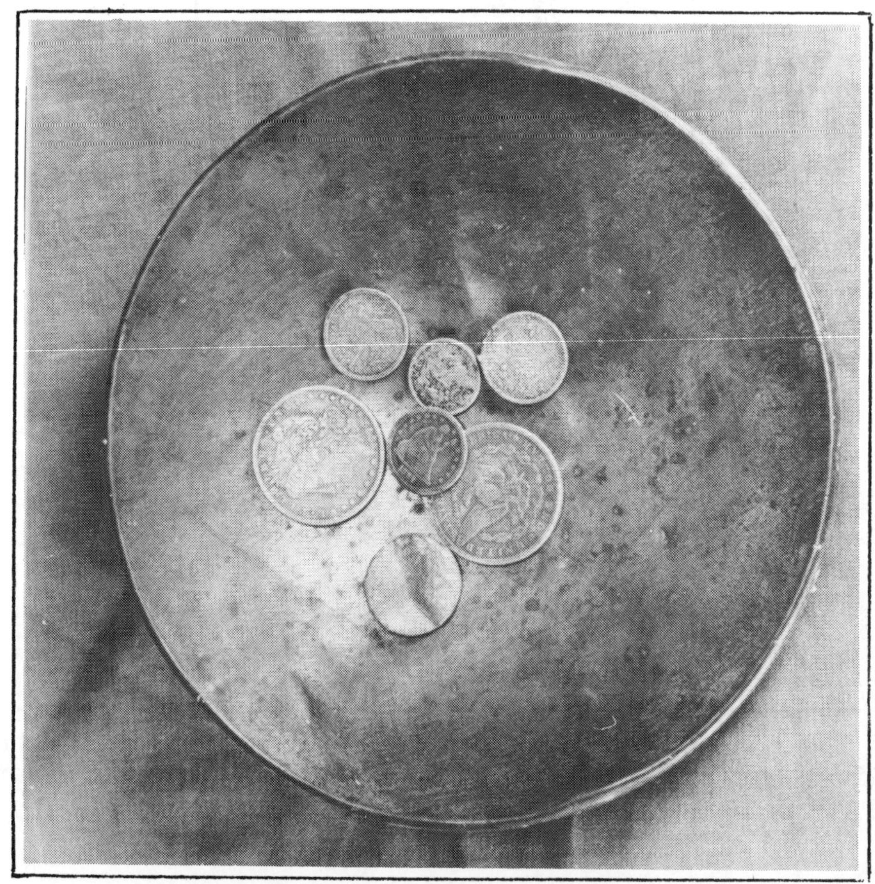

A handful of 114 coins recovered by the author in a ghost town.

quarry, it was located in the center of the tetrahedrite mineralized zone of northern Stevens County. The ore deposits in this part of the district usually occur in "vugs" or "chimneys;" generally rich narrow veins of high grade galena with a high silver content.

Several times during the years, Janni's crews had come upon veins of galena while taking out the limestone, but usually the veins were so narrow that they weren't worth mining. But in 1953 they came across an astonishingly rich chimney of ore. They had been mining the second level of the quarry when they suddenly broke into a galena vug. When encountered, it was approximately six feet by five feet - and it was solid galena! Among the crew; Alex Tyllia, Al Nelson, Hans Butte, Jack Murphy, Earl Midkiff, Raeder Carlson and a few others, nearly half of them were part-time prospectors and to a man they were very impressed with their unexpected discovery.

Shortly thereafter, Peter Janni arrived on the scene. The old man appraised the vug silently for a few minutes, then calmly said, "Follow

The old Janni quarry today. The "vug" was discovered by the crew when they were quarrying limestone. The chimney of ore, inexplicably, was later covered over by Janni's crew under orders from Peter Janni. The vug is still there according to the workers who were there.

her down, boys." And follow it they did, with a great deal more enthusiasm than they had ever shown when quarrying limestone.

Over the next few weeks nearly forty tons of exceptionally high grade galena was shipped to the C. M. & S. Company's lead refinery in nearby Trail. The shrew Janni kept the returns to himself, but his men had seen lots of high grade galena before and they knew that the ore contained a high percentage of silver.

Then a strange thing happened. After Janni's crew had opened up the vug and followed it down for just over fifteen feet. Peter Janni showed up early one morning, surveyed the shaft reflectively for a few minutes, then turned to his crew and said, "Cover the damn thing up!" His crew couldn't believe their ears. They had shipped close to forty tons of fabulous ore and the chimney, instead of decreasing at depth, was increasing in size - promising to become a significant ore body. Several of the old hands pleaded with Janni to let them follow it for a few more weeks or at least until the ore pinched out. But Janni was adamant, and reluctantly his men filled in the shaft and then levelled it off. When pressed for an explanation the old man only stated that, "Maybe some day we dig her up again."

Why Peter Janni covered up the chimney of ore remains a mystery to this day. There were many reasons advanced by the crew. Some said that he didn't want the mining interfering with his limestone operation. Others said that he didn't want his son Joe to know anything about it, because Joe, due home for the summer, had always had a strong interest in mining and might insist that they develop the showing. So the old man simply had the shaft covered up before Joe arrived.

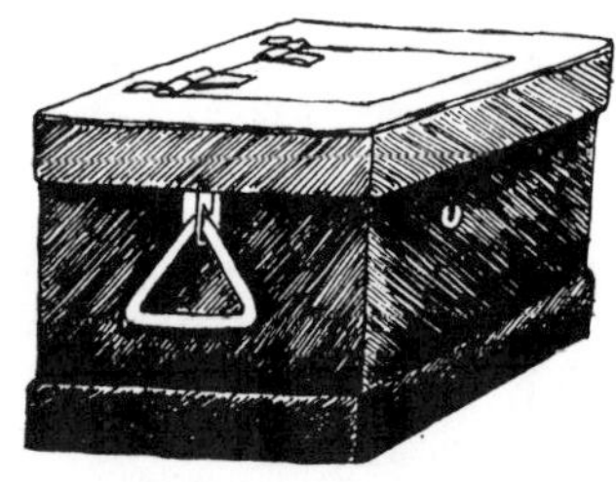

But none of these theories seem satisfactory. Peter Janni was an acute mining man with a considerable knowledge of lode mining and had previously invested heavily, and usually shrewdly, in various mines in northern Stevens County. He knew that that chimneys of high grade ore often occurred in the immediate area and that they usually carried a high percentage of silver. Why he suddenly abandoned the galena vug in his own quarry remains a mystery.

And according to three different sources in Northport, that rich galena chimney still lies buried under tons of limestone on the second level of Peter Janni's old quarry southwest of that historic town. It is possible, of course, that sometime during the intervening years that parties familiar with and particulars, returned surreptitiously and removed the remainder of the ore from that buried column.

But if they did, there is no visible sign of their activity. So, the ore is probably still there, somewhere under the limestone on the long abandoned upper level of the old quarry.

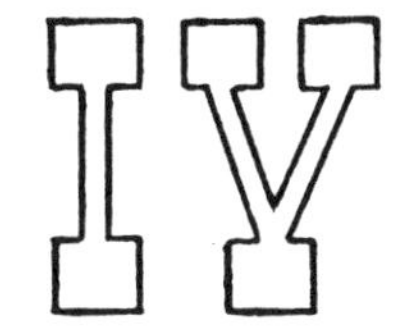

PEND OREILLE
COUNTY

INTRODUCTION

Pend Oreille County - This easternmost county in the state is cut by that river of yesterday, the Pend Oreille. The northern part of Pend Oreille county is, in many areas, little travelled even today. It was mining country in the last century and it still is.

There are places in this county where man hasn't traversed since the halcyon days of the mining era of the late 19th century; Hooknose Mountain, Russian Creek, Sullivan Creek, Lead Hill, Coyote Hill, Lead King Hills, Z Canyon and Divide Peak are generally quiet now although there was a time, decades ago, when every prospector in Pend Oreille county knew their names.

And towns like Metaline Falls and Ione are not like they used to be, in those years when lead ruled the upper part of this county. But there are unfrequented spots even today, places far off the usual and often travelled routes, places where the Pend Oreille of a century ago is not too far away and mines with names like Josephine, Bunker Hill, Grandview, Riverside, Lucky Strike and a host of others were considered world beaters.

Z Canyon before the Pend Oreille was tamed. This section of the river was breathtaking and was considered one of the wildest of all of the great rivers of the West. (Eastern Washington State Historical Soc.)

METALINE FALLS

The first site of Metaline Falls was on a flat on the north side of Sullivan Creek but that was when that prolific placer gold stream was still yielding gold by the pound.

In the 1890s, after significant discoveries of lead deposits had been made in the immediate vicinity, the old placer camp was abandoned and a new townsite established on a bench overlooking the Pend Oreille on the south side of the creek.

By 1910 a mining town of some consequence was drawing miners and prospectors by the score as its massive deposits of lead and zinc were proving to be immensely profitable. With more mines coming into production Metaline Falls quickly became the mining center of the county. Its main street was a hub of activity in those days with sternwheelers making regular trips down the river with passengers, machinery for the mines and freight. And those mines surrounding the town were prolific producers, several of them lasting for decades.

Metaline Falls is still there, and some of those buildings along Main Street have changed little since the early part of the century - when names like Rocky Reach, Poorman and Hanley were commonplace and sternwheelers like the Ione were still coming down the river.

The abandoned Metaline Falls placer gold camp as it appeared in 1900.
(photograph - Courtesy Eastern Washington State Historical Society)

Ione around the turn of the century. This little community lay south of Metaline Falls and was touted as the coming metropolis of northern Pend Oreille county. (Eastern Washington State Historical Society)

One of the early lead-zinc-silver mines in Pend Oreille County close to Metaline Falls. (Eastern Washington State Historical Society)

The sternwheeler Ione on the Pend Oreille river in the early days.
(Photograph - Courtesy Eastern Washington State Historical Society)

Townspeople gather in front of the newly constructed Washington Hotel in Metaline Falls. (Courtesy Eastern Washington State Historical Society)

PLACER GOLD

Discovered to be gold bearing in 1856, Pend Oreille County's renowned Sullivan Creek has yielded an estimated 11,900 troy ounces of coarse gold. Both white and Chinese miners toiled steadily on this stream for decades and did extremely well. This creek is still being worked by a handful of weekend placer miners.

<u>Pend Oreille River</u> ● This once magnificent river has been tamed by a series of dams stretching downriver almost to the Canadian border and thus much of the old placer ground has been inundated by flood waters. The mining history of this river, however, dates back to 1855. In that year placer gold was discovered on the bars of the Columbia north of old Fort Colville. As the prospectors moved upriver, they came across coarse gold at the mouth of a river which lay just over the border on the British side. This wild and treacherous river they called "Clark's Fork," although it was, in fact, the Pend Oreille. As they slowly and carefully made their way up this watercourse they struck "ounce a day" diggings - the placer miner's dream. A short-lived but bloody war with the Indians on the lower part of the river slowed, but failed to halt either their mining or their steady ascent of the river. Finally, the river, slowly arcing southward crossed back into the United States. And these hardy argonauts found magnificent ground, all the way from the border upriver just over ten miles to the mouth of a stream which they called Sullivan. Unfortunately, the only placer ground available today is a stretch of barely one mile between the Boundary Dam and the Canadian border.

Prospects: Generally poor. The best ground is underwater.

The Pend Oreille river below Boundary Dam. This section of the river produced considerable quantities of gold in the early years. A cabin, built by prospectors nearly half a century ago, still stands close by that once vaunted gold river.

TREASURES & LOST MINES

Sullivan Creek, just upstream from the "Sullivan Creek Find" area. Barely one hundred feet from this point, a number of old coins have been found and are still turning up - their point of origin remains unknown.

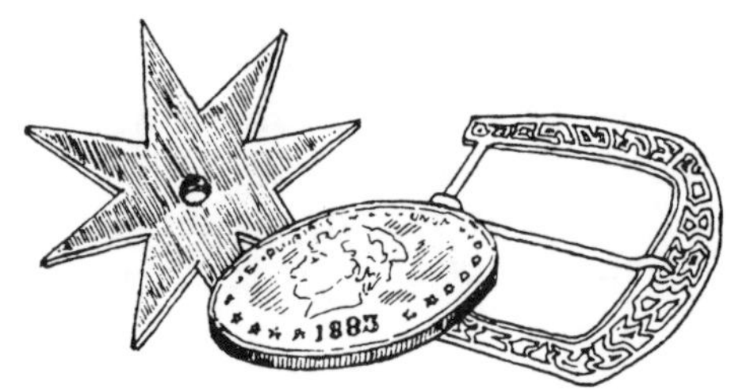

SULLIVAN CREEK MYSTERY

Steve Story is an interesting man. He is fascinated by the history of Pend Oreille County and he knows once famous Sullivan Creek like nobody else does. And he should because he has prospected it all the way from the North Fork down to its mouth where it joins the historic Pend Oreille river. Of all the placer creeks in the county, Sullivan Creek is by far the most illustrious and has yielded many thousands of ounces of coarse gold to generations of placer miners. They found the royal metal in quantity in many places along this stream, especially in the slate bedrock near its mouth.

And that is the section of the creek where Steve Story has spent the majority of his time prospecting. Sometimes he snipes the bedrock crevices and occasionally he uses a small portable dredge to scour the bottom of the creek.

He lives in nearby Metaline Falls and his work allows him ample spare time for prospecting. He's done reasonably well, considering the creek has been mined for well over a century. He has found close to a troy pound of gold but in the summer of 1977 he came across two finds in close proximity to each other which may or may not be related.

Steve Story with just over seven ounces of coarse gold from Sullivan creek. Most of the gold was recovered from just below the canyon.

One day, when he was dredging just below the powerhouse, close to the south bank of the creek, he uncovered a silver dollar, dated 1890. In the next few minutes he found some more coins; two old nickels, a 1900 mercury dime and another silver dollar, dated 1896. He had found placer tools and even some tin cups in his dredging operations before but never so many coins together. Contemplating this puzzle, he moved his dredging operations downstream, between the bridge and the mouth of the stream. And two weeks later he struck another bonanza, again on the south side. He was cleaning up between two boulders when he saw a heavy gold chain glinting under the water. He reached down and picked it up. He was amazed when he noticed that it was almost 18" in length and was marked 18k. It was a valuable find. Darkness was closing when he made his discovery so he called it a day. The next morning he was back again, carefully scanning the bedrock. He was almost prepared to give up when he saw a gold watch lying in the gravel. He picked up his glittering prize and examined it - it was a solid gold watch, 21k. It had undoubtedly once been attached to the gold chain he had found the day before, not two feet away.

It was a strange summer for Steve Story; two puzzling and fairly valuable discoveries on Sullivan creek within several hundred feet of each other. He has never solved the puzzle and it's doubtful that he ever will - that historic creek guards its secrets well.

The coins were found just above the bridge and the gold chain and the gold watch were found several hundred feet downstream from the bridge. The mystery remains unsolved.

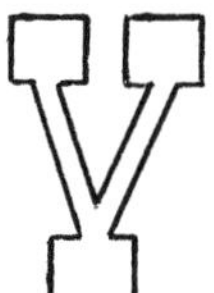

CHELAN COUNTY

INTRODUCTION

Chelan County - Long considered to be one of the most scenic of all of the counties east of the Cascades, this region not only has a wide and intriguing history, but in many ways it is little changed since the early 1890s.

Lake Chelan remains a breathtakingly beautiful expanse of water, penetrated only by lakeboats for much of its length. Old Holden, that once famous mining camp which yielded a Croesus hoard of gold, silver and other metals for so many years, is no more. But Stehekin presides yet over the head of the lake, as it has for so many years.

There is little mining activity on those once vaunted streams by that lake, creeks like Railroad and Cascade, but there are places in this county where the windows into the past remain almost unclouded. One of those enclaves of yesteryear is the Blewett Pass region in the southern part of the county. Here, along placer creeks like Peshastin, Shaser, Ingalls and half a dozen other streams and in the surrounding hills the mining years are only a step away. Old Blewett, that colorful camp of the turn of the century has vanished but old stamp mills, forgotten cemeteries, ancient arrastras and other signs of those glory days remain behind. This is Chelan County at its best.

A memorable photograph of early Chelan by L. D. Lindsley, one of the pioneer photographers of the Lake Chelan region.
(photograph - Special Collections Division University of Washington)

GHOST TOWNS

A mining camp called "Old Blewett," in the Blewett Pass area of Chelan County - circa 1905. A stamp mill and about twenty other buildings were scattered along the narrow Pashastin creek canyon. At that time several hundred men, both placer miners and lode miners, were in the immediate area. Much of this historic old mining camp has now vanished, a victim of highway construction through the center of the old site. The area, however, remains one of the most fascinating parts in Chelan County.
(Photograph courtesy of Department of Natural Resources)

and MINING TOWNS

CHELAN

They say that Chelan is one of the most beautiful places in the state - and perhaps it is.

The earliest settlers were Chinese placer miners who were mining the bars on the nearby Columbia as late as the 1870s. They remained, gleaning an arduous living from the gravels until they were driven out by the local Indians. By 1881 the United States Army had established Camp Chelan and several years later the first settlers started coming in. "Hayman" Farrar was probably the first but he was followed by men like Captain A. S. Burbank, J. F. Woodring, Joel Treadwell, James H. Chase, J. L. Weythman, R. A. Brown and a handful of others. Among the other early arrivals was William Sanders, a sometimes prospector who was convinced that the upper regions of Lake Chelan held vast mineral riches. He teamed up with an unlikely individual named Henry Dumke, a somewhat confused wanderer who was also a part time prospector. Their first expedition was dogged by ill fortune. In attempting to prospect in difficult terrain they managed to lose their burro, their food and their equipment. Dumke later achieved some local notoriety by building a sawmill in which the wheel ran backwards. But Sanders and Dumke were finally proven right when mineral discoveries were made on Cascade and

A few of the boys on the upper reaches of Lake Chelan around 1910. In those years the Chelan area was considered sure-fire mining country. (photograph - Special Collections Division, University of Washington)

Two unnamed cowboys in their "woolies" on the shores of Lake Chelan.
(Photograph - Special Collections Division, University of Washington)

An early L. D. Lindsley photograph of Chelan during its formative years. Lindsley, a pioneer photographer, concentrated on the Chelan region and left hundreds of fine photographs of the area.
(Photograph - Special Collections Division, University of Washington)

Railroad creeks and beyond the head of the lake. Eventually the great Holden mine, ultimately to become one of the greatest producers in the state, came into production and provided millions of dollars worth of precious metals during its long life.

"Chelan Jim" and Henry Dumke are long gone and so is the renowned Holden mine but the town of Chelan still guards the foot of that most memorable lake as it has for well over a century.

And the entire area is one of the most splendid regions in Chelan County, unsurpassed in natural beauty. It is little wonder that early photographers like L. D. Lindsley spent most of their spare moments in the region, capturing the haunting splendor of Lake Chelan.

The renowned Holden mine near the head of Railroad creek.

A classic photograph of an open stage leaving Chelan in 1907. On the face of the cliff behind the stage is a sign advertising the Chelan Hotel. (Courtesy Eastern Washington State Historical Society, Cheney Coles Museum)

OLD BLEWETT

It had the reputation as the most violent mining camp in Chelan County and that reputation was well earned. It was called "The Camp," in the early years and it was a hell-raiser from the beginning.

When placer miners found placer gold in quantity along Peshastin Creek a rush of prospectors flooded into the district. Among them was a certain John Shafer who located the first quartz claim in the area in 1874. Almost at the same time Sam Culver located the Pole Pick and Hummingbird claims on the south side of the gulch which soon came to be known as "Culver Gulch."

When the veins proved to carry magnificent amounts of "free gold" in the quartz the gulch was stampeded as word of the richness of the ore circulated throughout the territory. By 1878 a stamp mill had been erected to process the ore and soon after a few permanent shacks were thrown up for the miners. In 1879, after the lead was found to extend both east and west, a wagon road was built to connect the camp to the outside and Cle Elum. With three or four arrastras and the stamp mill the production from Culver Gulch began to rise as mines like the Pole Pick, Blackjack, Peshastin, Tip Top and others contributed ore.

Detail of the hotel in Old Blewett. The region nearby was both placer gold and lode gold country and has been mined more or less steadily for well over a century by generations of miners.

By the 1890s companies like the Blewett Company, which produced $60,000 in bullion in 1896, were engaging more and more miners and the camp began to increase its dimensions. Two years later it was home to nearly 100 people, most of them lode miners. There was a busy hotel, a general store and post office, a twenty stamp mill, a livery stable, two saloons and several dozen shacks for the miners.

Some of the high-grade ore coming from the mines was truly mind boggling - in certain instances it ran upwards of 500 ounces per ton; or more than $225,000.00, in today's market, for approximately a cubic yard of ore. It was the spectacular nature of this gold laden quartz which proved to be the lure for so many miners. It was a region where a single pocket might well yield a king's ransom in gold, and because of that the mines were highly prized and jealously guarded - powderkeg ingredients which led to fueds, gunplay and occasionally murder. This explosive atmosphere of the 1890s culminated in more than one bloody affray, the most celebrated of which was the murder of Bill Donahue by Tom Johnson over the ownership of the Culver Company, but that wasn't the only time guns were brought into play - Old Blewett was noted for its rough characters and free wheeling ways. Certainly one of the most unusual transfers of a mine from one owner to another took place when Henry Earnest, Thaddeus Neubauer and Peter Anderson sat down to play a

A hand mortar and pestle used for crushing high grade quartz ore and recovering the gold and a miner's helmet with attached carbide lamp. Both items were used by lode miners in the Blewett area.

friendly game of poker. Unfortunately, as the game progressed and the gold eagles and double eagles began to pile up in front of an elated Newbauer, things started to get out of hand between the three friends. But the longer they played, the luckier Newbauer got. Finally, in the small hours of the morning Earnest got four of a kind, a very good hand indeed - and almost unbeatable. He bet half of his dwindling pile of coins; Newbauer met the bet and raised. The cunning Earnest, positive that he held the winning hand, saw the raise and then placed the last of his coins in the pot. His opponent hesitated, then saw the raise. There was now several thousand dollars in gold coins in the pot, but Earnest, probably the finest poker player in camp, had no more money, while Newbauer, not nearly as skilled, still had several glinting and impressive stacks in front of him. Earnest, eyeing them greedily, was determined to win that pile. When Newbauer called for a card, Earnest was astounded - his opponent was drawing against four of a kind! In a moment Earnest sensed his opportunity; he offered to bet his mine, the Lucky Queen, against Newbauer's glittering stacks of gold. And to his utter amazement, his opponent agreed. Earnest dealt the card and bet his mine. Newbauer peered at the card and called, pushing his stacks of coins into the pot. Earnest proudly turned over his hand, exposing his four of a kind, and reached for the gold coins. Newbauer, grinning

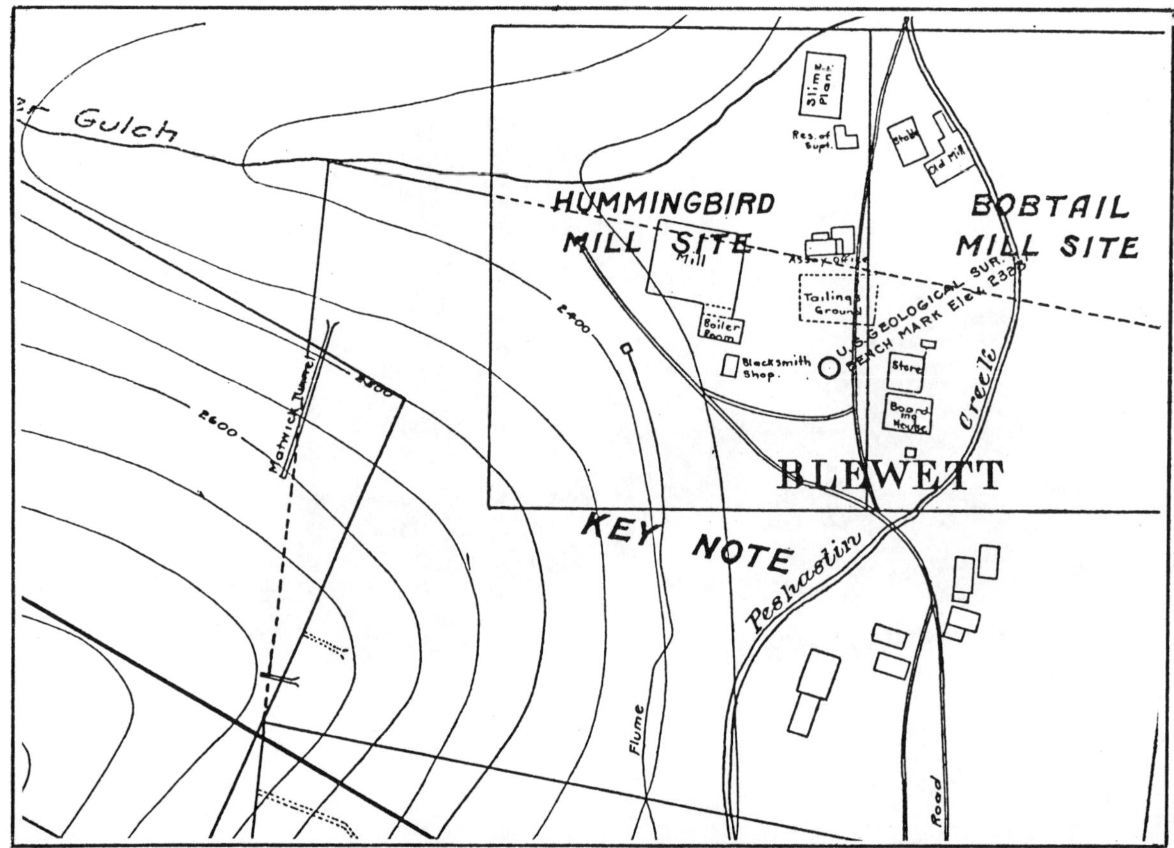

An early sketch of the townsite of Old Blewett showing the Bobtail and Hummingbird mill sites, Peshastin Creek and other buildings sites.

broadly, turned over his own hand. Earnest glanced at it, then stared in utter dismay - spread out before him was the best hand in poker, a royal flush! Newbauer, holding the ten, jack, king and ace of hearts, had to draw the queen of hearts and Earnest had dealt that exact card to him. Thus the Lucky Queen mine changed hands, by pure coincidence to a player who had drawn the lucky queen!

But Old Blewett, after those high-grade veins petered out, was to fade into oblivion. Eventually, after the highway connecting Cle Elum with Wenatchee was completed, almost every sign of that colorful camp was obliterated by blacktop.

There are still signs of those halcyon times though; tunnels and shafts and abandoned workings, including the ruins of the stamp mill and the remains of a remarkably preserved arrastra close by Peshastin creek - mute evidence of those days when Old Blewett was alive.

Some of seven gold and diamond rings found by the author in an early western mining camp. Also screened out were over 100 gold and silver coins, many of them dated prior to 1900. The Blewett Pass region has yielded four known caches of coins or other valuables to date. Many of the numerous isolated cabin sites are still worth investigating. The early prospector or miner, trusting only his own devices, often cached his valuables, including gold and silver specie, near or in his cabin.

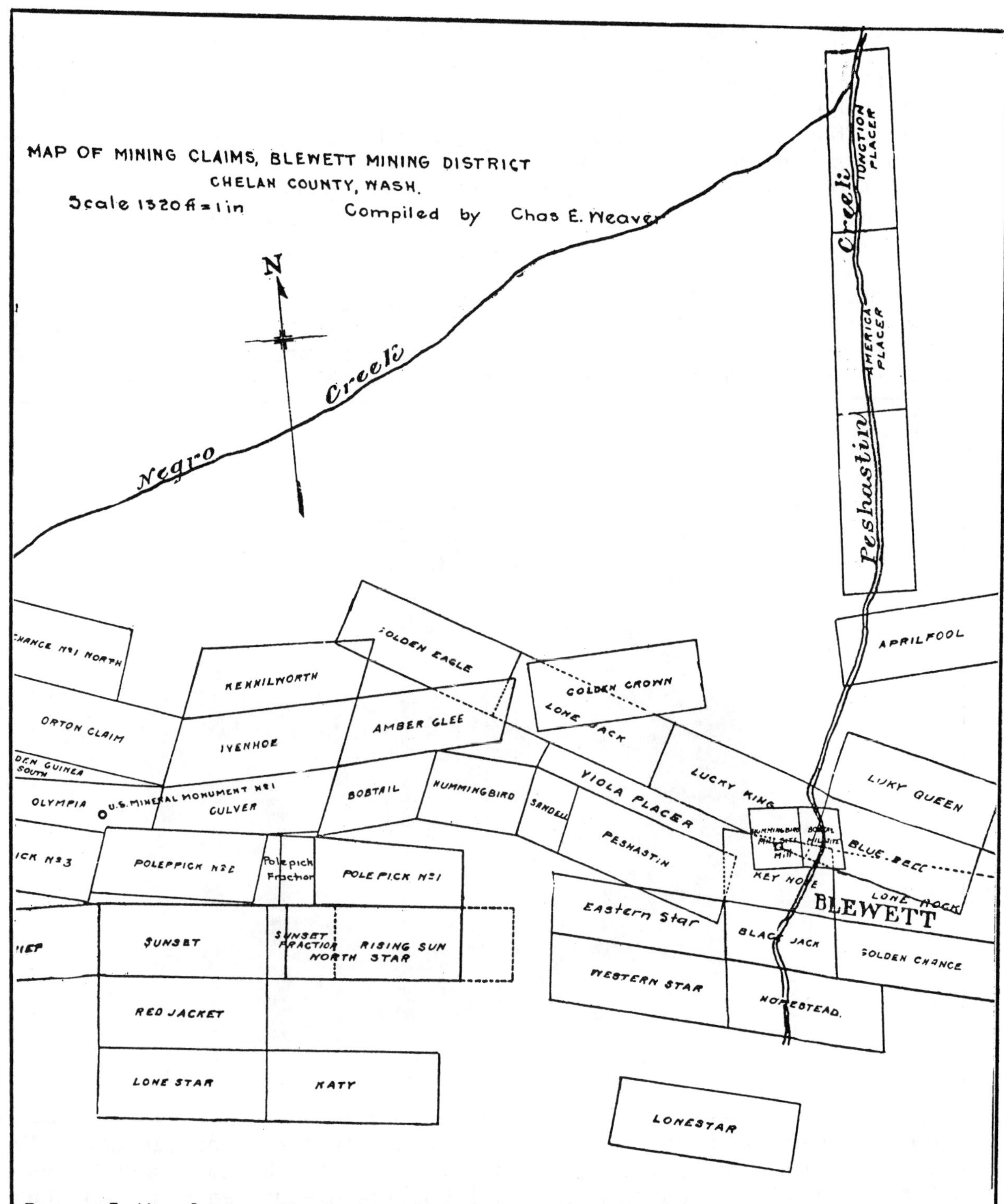

Some of the lode and placer claims around the old camp of Blewett are shown on the map above. Compiled by Charles Weaver, probably in 1896 or 1897, many of the renowned claims of Culver Gulch are shown. With mines like the Pole Pick, Lucky Queen, Hummingbird, Bobtail and a dozen more high grade, free milling gold properties, Old Blewett, for many years, had the reputation as one of the richest mining camps in the state.

PLACER GOLD

The original arrastra by Penhastin creek, near the vanished mining camp of Blewett. Barely a hundred yards downstream lies the gaunt remains of an old mill while all through the rest of this part of the Blewell Pass region tailings, tunnels and shafts attest to the hectic activity which took place in this part of Chelan County in the late 1800s.

Deep Creek ● This little known stream is a tributary of the Chiwawa river and flows into it about four miles east of Wenatchee Lake. This creek was mined near its mouth in 1890 when some generally fine gold was recovered. It has been almost unworked since that date.

Prospects: Never a good placer gold region, Deep creek did produce some flour gold but not much of it. Generally considered a poor area for placer gold. Don't count on it for coarse gold.

Entiat River ● A generally unpublicized placer river in Chelan County which rises in the mountains south of Lake Chelan and flows into the Columbia river at the town of Entiat. State Geologist George Bethune reported in 1891 that there were "about 60 (miners) on the Entiat." A perusal of later reports indicates a lack of activity on the river and it is probable that those early miners cleaned up most of the placer gold along the Entiat.

Prospects: A patient placer man might be well advised to prospect along the Entiat, especially along the sections where the bedrock is visible. Even then it should not be expected to produce much more than very limited quantities of flour gold. Interesting but probably a poor bet.

The Entiat, shown here, was worked in the 1890s by nearly 60 miners. It was, however, a spotty and generally poor gold river. Generally a fine gold river with occasional bedrock sections.

Icicle Creek ● This significant stream rises in the Cascades in the southwestern corner of Chelan County, almost due west of Leavenworth. Although there has been little activity on this creek for decades, the state records state that the gold output prior to 1890 was "reportedly considerable." Unfortunately even dedicated prospectors would have a rough time on this creek because of its high water, huge boulders and numerous canyons.

Prospects: The Icicle does flow through mineralized country but it has never been a noted producer of placer gold and it is unlikely that it will become one at this late date.

Ingalls Creek ● A little placer gold was produced near the mouth of this stream where it enters Peshastin creek from the west. Most of the gold was recovered on the lower reaches of this stream.

Prospects: Not good as it has been thoroughly prospected from its mouth upstream for miles. Many other placer creeks look better.

Mad River ● This river is the southern fork of the Entiat river. The Mad has yielded some fine gold since the late 1880s, but never a great amount. 1898 was probably its best year and it wasn't spectacular.

Prospects: Not exciting, although exposed bedrock sections could be checked out to determine whether or not flood gold is being deposited. Don't expect any real surprises from this river.

Prince Creek ● A creek which flows into Lake Chelan from the northeastern side of the lake. This stream yielded some quantities of fine flour gold to some miners, mostly during the 1930s.

Prospects: Prince creek was never a noted producer of placer gold. It is unlikely that any deposits of significance will be found at the present time as it has already been reasonably well prospected.

Railroad Creek ● Another stream which runs into Lake Chelan that has yielded placer gold. Discovered around 1889, this creek has given up some generally fine gold. The exact production is unrecorded but it is not considered great. The ground was mined from its mouth on upstream for almost a mile to a place once called "Dan's Camp."

Prospects: Not encouraging unless you're satisfied with flour gold and lean diggings. Railroad creek is certainly not one of the better placer creeks in the county but the scenery is spectacular, like most of that Lake Chelan country.

Ruby Creek ● Discovered in the early 1860s, this stream yielded some placer gold near its mouth. Hand mined at first, it was hydraulicked in the later 1890s by miners like the Lynch brothers, Riley Eisenhour and Thomas Medhurst.

Prospects: The best ground, near the mouth, has been well mined by generations of placer miners. Some fine colors but little else of any consequence. A marginal placer stream now. There are much better gold creeks in the Blewett Pass area than this one.

Scotty Creek ● Also in the Blewett Pass district. A tributary of the Peshastin, it has been a generally lackluster placer creek. There are a few places along this stream where gold is still found, but it is a insignificant producer.

Prospects: Although Scotty creek rises in mineralized country, the general consensus of this stream is that the deposits are both sparse and difficult to locate. It might be wise to bypass this creek unless you are willing to take a chance on generally poor gooodd.

Shaser Creek ● Discovered in the 1860s, this stream is also a branch of Peshastin creek. Ignored during the discovery years because of its reputation for generally fine gold, it has come back into its own in the past few years as recreational panners try their luck. There is a fairly large basin which is drained by South Shaser, Middle Shaser and North Shaser creeks. The most productive ground, which is not rich by any means, is located along the lower parts of the creeks.

An overshot waterwheel in the Swauk Creek - Peshastin Creek region. (Special Collections Div. University of Washington Library)

Negro Creek ● This is a tributary of Peshastin creek which was found to be gold bearing in or around 1860 reputedly by miners coming back from the Fraser river diggings in British Columbia. One of the placer men, a negro, took out 75 ounces of coarse gold and nuggets from the mouth of this stream where it enters Peshastin creek, thus giving the creek its name. The stream continued to yield well over the next four decades with the best results coming from claims near its mouth. Gold was, however, also found in decreasing but occasionally paying amounts upstream for almost six miles. This creek has been exhaustively mined and has surrendered an estimated 2,000 or more ounces since its discovery almost one hundred and thirty years ago.

Prospects: Although Negro creek has been a renowned placer creek, the best ground has been heavily mined. It is unlikely that any large deposits or old channels will be discovered at this late date. It has a rich history but there are better placer creeks in the Blewett Pass region.

Peshastin Creek ● Undoubtedly the most prodigious producer of placer gold in Chelan County. This stream was bonanza ground all through the discovery years and was yielding up to 3 ounces a square yard as late as the 1890s to miners like the Bloom brothers, Frank Holley, John H.

The mouth of Negro Creek as it enters the Peshastin. This noted placer gold stream has produced prodigious amounts of coarse gold, most of it mined during the discovery years from its mouth upstream for 2 miles.

Snyder, J. H. Crawford and scores more. Fourteen miles of this famous stream yielded an estimated total of somewhat more than 12,000 ounces from the 1860s to the 1920s. There were a number of high old channels which surrendered significant amounts of coarse gold and nuggets to a great many placer miners. These ancient high channels often required either shafts or tunnels to mine the bedrock. The richest section of Peshastin was from about ½ mile below the mouth of Negro creek and on upstream for nearly six miles. The lower part of Peshastin, below the canyon, was extensively dredged by a commercial dredge years ago. The old timers also hydraulicked in various sections and the entire gold-bearing part of the stream has been extensively hand mined. Peshastin creek was well known for its coarse gold and nuggets although nuggets weighing more than an ounce were rare, a great many slugs of under ½ ounce have been recovered.

Prospects: Peshastin is solidly claimed all along its upper section and these claims are tightly held and well posted. Despite its past it is still yielding some good gold from time to time. The first dredgers on the creek did extremely well and the obvious places have been gone over several times since then. Although it is a formidable job to find good ground today some of the miners scattered along this stream are still recovering interesting amounts of gold. To get on Peshastin now is difficult unless an agreement is made with a claim holder.

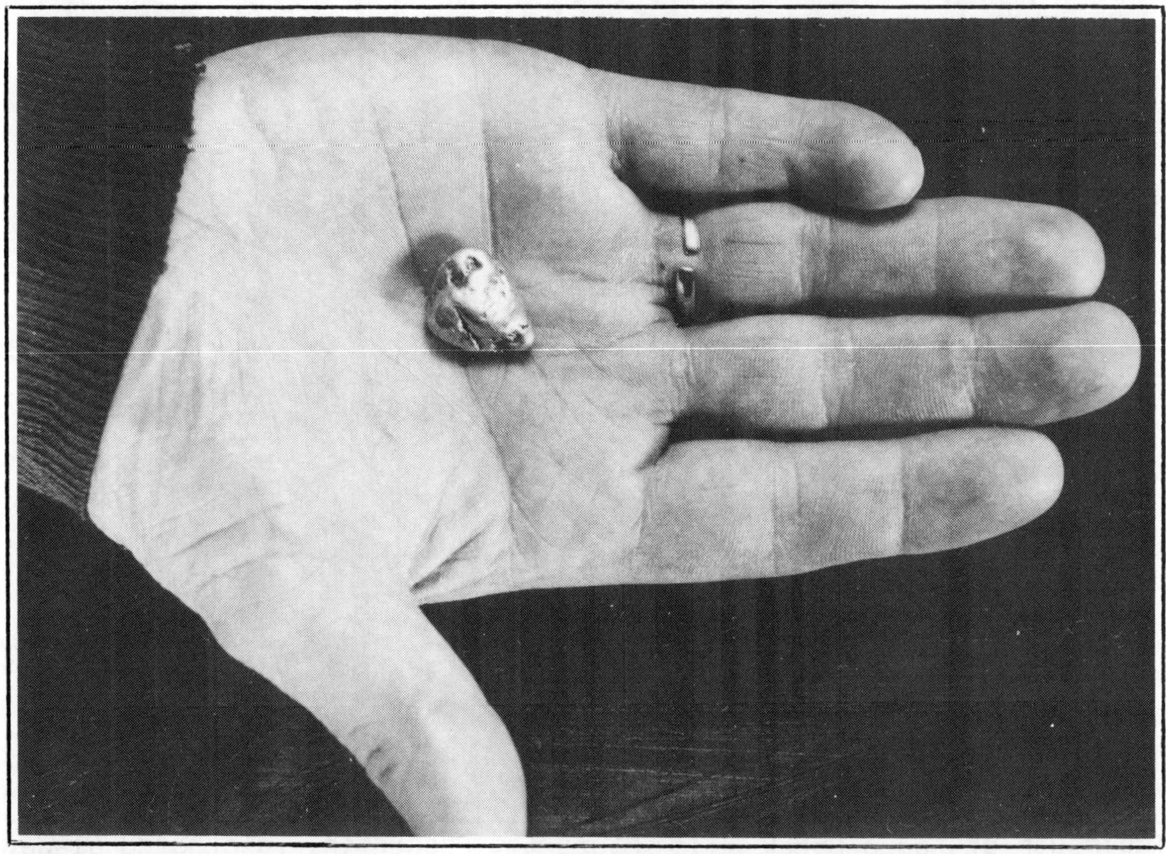

Three-quarter ounce nuggets like the one in the author's hand weren't rare on Peshastin during the discovery years, but they are today.

Prospects:

There are some possibilities. Interesting topography with remote chances of locating old channels, although they would probably not be very rich. A fascinating piece of country.

Stehekin River ● At the head of Lake Chelan. This river was found to carry gold in 1888. There are some placers near its mouth and more up towards its headwaters. Evidently a considerable amount of placer gold was recovered in the first three or four years of mining. In 1891, a report by George A. Bethune, the State Geologist, mentioned that "120 miners were working on the Stehekin...." The precise amount of placer gold produced along the river was not recorded but was rumored to be considerable. There was some mining in the 1930s, mostly on the bars, but not much since then.

Prospects: Could be. A reasonable length of this river does carry some generally fine gold. Worth looking at for fine gold only.

Wenatchee River ● A surprising amount of gold has been recovered from several different locations along this river. One of these spots was about a mile west of Leavenworth, close to the mouth of Steep creek, another was on the south bank of the Wenatchee just about a mile west of Dryden. In this latter location Keene and Benjamin of Seattle were successful in an operation in the 1890s when they sluiced thousands of cubic yards from an old buried channel downriver from Peshastin creek. It is estimated that this operation recovered hundreds of ounces from ground that sometimes averaged more than 1 pennyweight a yard.

Prospects: Better than average probably. The Wenatchee has produced a significant amount of gold down through the years and the chances of locating other good patches of ground on this river are reasonable. A sharp prospector might be well advised to stay close to those discoveries of the 1890s. Still an interesting river for placer miners.

VI
KITTITAS COUNTY

INTRODUCTION

Kittitas County - Fleeting images of the past still hover close by in this historic county where names like Liberty, Roslyn, Cle Elum and a handful of other mining camps of old come to mind. Those prospectors of other years, men like Tom Meagher, Gus Nelson, Clarence Virden and a legion of others have long vanished from their old haunts but those storied creeks; Swauk, Williams and Baker, although long past the high production years continue to grudgingly surrender their golden tithe.

Travel along the overgrown trails on rivers like the Cle Elum or the Teanaway and you follow in the footsteps of the pathfinders of the 1880s and 1890s who penetrated into the far reaches in their unceasing quest for the motherlode. And remnants of their passing may still be seen; long abandoned tunnels, broken down arrastras, deserted cabins, tailings, a lonely grave or some other reminder that they were there.

This region has many forgotten corners, remote places which the uninitiated seldom reach, but they're there, there in the unfrequented and shadowy canyons of the Cascades, there in the Liberty triangle and there in the upper Cle Elum and beyond. From the magnificence of the high country to the secrets of the Swauk this is an unforgettable and uncommon region - the county they still call Kittitas.

An abandoned road grader east of Liberty. There are many reminders of the past all through this part of Kittitas County.

GHOST TOWNS

Original false-fronted stores line once busy Pennsylvania Avenue in old Roslyn. For decades this fascinating town was the center of the empire of coal in Kittitas County. Although those glory days have passed, the town has retained that turn of the century mood, one of the last places in the state where nearly all of the original buildings remain standing. Roslyn is unique.

and MINING TOWNS

LIBERTY

It's the oldest continually inhabited mining camp in the state. In well over a century its miners have produced more than three and a quarter tons of placer gold; making it the most renowned placer gold camp in Washington. It has had several names but its present name, an honored and historic name - is Liberty.

When gold in quantity was discovered on Swauk creek in 1868, the placer men soon found that its eastern tributary, Williams creek, was even richer than its parent. By the 1880s, the little camp beside the creek had changed its name from "Williams Creek," to "Meaghersville," after Thomas Meagher, one of the earliest and most successful miners on the creek. At that time there was a camp called "Liberty," on Swauk creek. By the turn of the century, however, the shallow diggings along Swauk were almost exhausted and that camp was abandoned.

In 1912, when the deep ground of Williams creek was producing a steady stream of gold, the post office was moved from old Liberty to Meaghersville on Williams creek, and that camp's name, in accordance with post office regulations, was changed to "Liberty." So the present Liberty, which has carried three different names, still stands beside famous Williams creek as it has for more than 120 years.

An old prospector's cabin on the north side of the road in Liberty.

A miner's cabin on Boulder Cr. in the Liberty region.

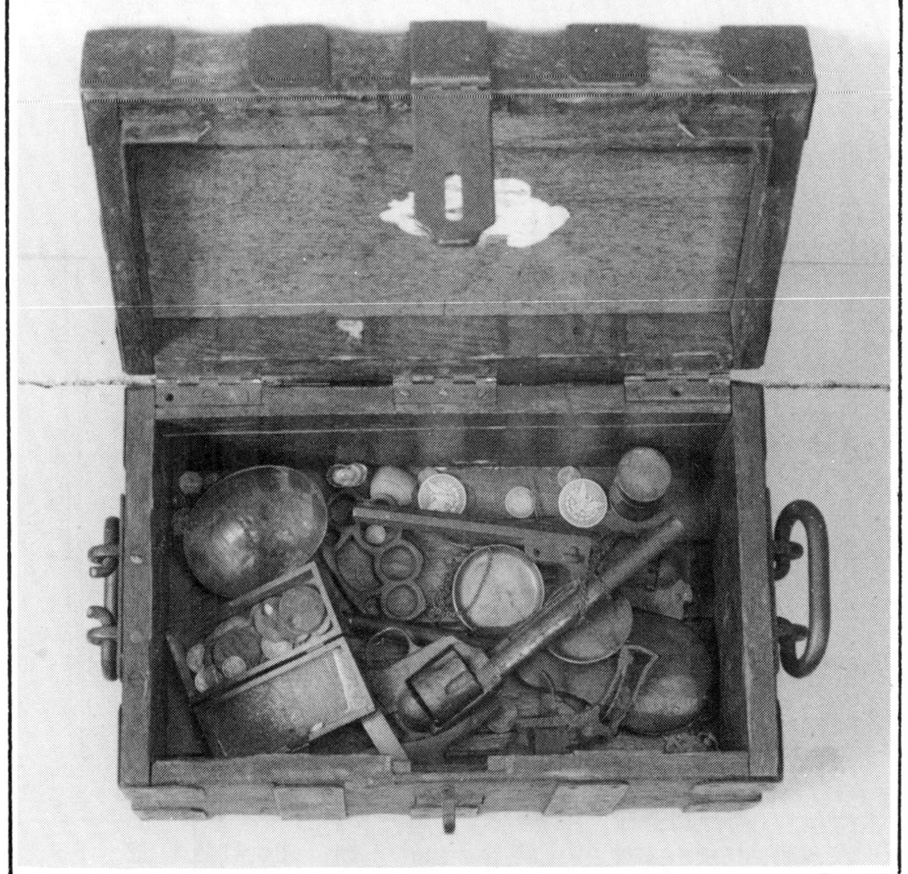

Guns, coins and other material from the ghost towns in an old strongbox.

ROSLYN

In many ways it is a classic mining town and one of a dwindling number of historic towns in Washington which have somehow retained a certain indefineable mood that few other towns possess.

Turn west onto Pennsylvania Avenue and the Roslyn of old stands before you. There, along that attractive avenue, more than a dozen false-front, turn of the century stores, complete with fading wood - still stand. This old town has character to spare.

In 1886 two prospectors, Nez Jensen and an itinerant blacksmith named George Virden, the latter eventually to become a famous miner in the Liberty area, found a mountain of coal southeast of Cle Elum Lake. At the time there was great demand for coal because the era of railroad building had begun, and the railroads were looking for coal, especially the Northern Pacific. A consortium soon took over the vast holdings of Jensen and Virden and by the end of the year the Roslyn coal mines were in production. Cluse by, a fledgling mining town began to take shape. And it was a rough camp in those years, populated by hundreds of hardnosed coal miners who played as hard as they worked. Before long the camp became a town - and what a town it was. Saloons dominated the business section and most of them were doing a booming

The Roslyn Cemetery is probably one of the most unique cemeteries in the entire West. Carefully segregated into nearly twenty different and separate areas - it is unusual.

trade as their raucous customers were jammed in elbow to elbow. Many of the diverse nationalities patronized only saloons owned by their own countrymen, thus the Italians, Poles, Lithuanians, Croatians and other linguistic groups all had their favorite drinking places. The boardwalks, in those days, were crowded with miners, many seeking the usual raw diversions of all rough edged mining towns; dalliances with women of questionable virtue, high stakes games of chance, no quarter bare knuckle fights or any other entertainment which was offered.

And it was an exciting town with more than its share of drama and

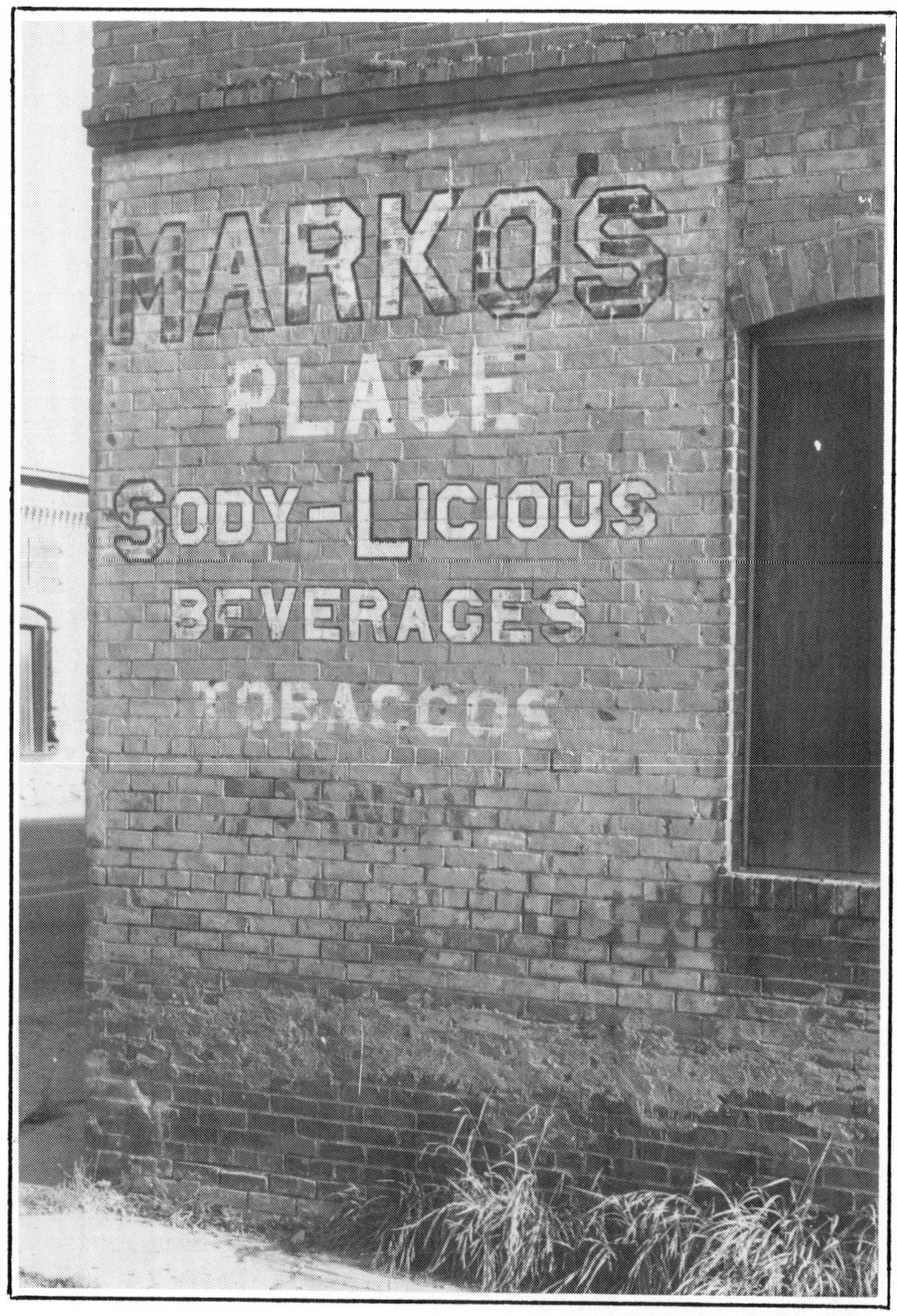

Marko's sign has faded a bit over the decades and the store is now closed.

tragedy. On May 9th, 1892, a disastrous explosion ripped through the tunnels of the No. 1 mine, leaving in its wake 45 dead miners and a town in mourning. On the 24th of September in that same year another disaster occurred, this time a financial one when the Snipes Bank was held up by three strangers who escaped with more than $20,000.00. The economic reverberations shook Roslyn and the depositors of the bank, many of whom had their life's savings in its vault. A subsequent trial found one Cal Hale guilty although the general feeling in Roslyn was that the four McCarty brothers and a certain Ras Lewis had pulled off the job, and the evidence was convincing. The repurcussions were far reaching, especially for the main participants. The unfortunate Hale, protesting his innocence to the last, was packed off to an asylum for the insane, where he spent many years. Old Ben Snipes, the prominent owner of the bank and a substantial citizen of the county, never did recover from the losses although the bank managed to stagger along to 1893, when the depression of that year closed its doors forever, marking the beginning of the end for Snipes' far flung empire. The four McCarty brothers left the district. Some years later their careers were rather abruptly terminated when three of the four; George, Fred and Tom, were killed while attempting to rob a bank in Delta, Colorado. Ras Lewis,

A hose reel near the firehall in Roslyn today. This is one of several hose reels in this historic town. Roslyn is also the departure point for the Cle-Elum River country and the old mining district far to the north. Indeed this historic and fascinating old town with its unique "Old West" cemetery, its scores of turn-of-the-century buildings and interesting byways is gradually becoming noted as one of those towns where history seems to have stood still.

considered the kingpin behind the robbery, survived and even prospered. He drifted into Utah and there, using the name "Matt Warner," he became a dedicated and long serving lawman, ultimately ending his days as a respected and honored citizen.

But these were only temporary setbacks. By 1901 the population had reached the 3,500 mark, production at the mines passed 1,000,000 tons for the first time and the town was booming. The ROSLYN NEWS and later the CASCADE MINER boosted the prospects of Roslyn and for almost two more decades the town prospered. Finally, during the 1920s, the demand for coal began to slacken off and by the end of that decade Roslyn was beginning to slip. Empty premises and shuttered windows reflected the hard times and streets with colorful names like Utah, Montana, Dakota and Idaho no longer resounded to the steady tramp of miners coming off shift as the company began to lay off alarming numbers of men. But the town survived, not many coal towns do, but Roslyn did.

Today the Fourth of July parades are a far cry from the old days when the town was on the rise. But there are still reminders of those days. A walk through the Roslyn cemetery, with its carefully segregated and posted sections, is a walk with history because this burying ground is one of the most unique cemeteries in the West. And wander through the downtown, especially at dust - then the visions of the Roslyn of old are never far away.

One of many abandoned stores in the business district of Roslyn. This building, like many others lends an old town atmosphere to the town. In many respects Roslyn has retained a special feeling that few other towns in the area have.

PLACER GOLD

Sluiceboxes lie abandoned near a deserted mining operation on Williams creek in the historic Swauk Creek Mining District near old Liberty. Williams creek and nearby Swauk creek were the premier gold producers in Kittitas County and are still considered to be the richest placer creeks in the state. Since their discovery in the 1860s, estimates of their production range from 80,000 to 125,000 troy ounces of raw gold, a staggering total of somewhere between 2½ and 3¼ tons of gold.

Baker Creek ● Another of the renowned gold creeks in the old Liberty district. This stream was found to be gold bearing in 1868 and holds the records for producing the largest nuggets in Washington; a huge slug weighing more than six pounds troy and another which tilted the scales at more than four and a half pounds troy. The best diggings on Baker were near its mouth where it joins Swauk creek. William Ford, J. C. Pike and a host of other placer men made their reputations and their fortunes on this amazing creek. Mined heavily for many years, it probably produced in excess of 25,000 ounces in well under half a mile of diggings. The origin of the placer gold is local veins.

Prospects: A limited patch of ground is presently being worked by local placer miners and it, like its neighboring creeks, Williams and Swauk, is heavily claimed. Not much chance getting onto ground along this creek.

Big Salmon La Sac ● Another eastern tributary of the Cle Elum river which carries some fine gold. Worked by the Chinese for a limited and unrecorded time.

Prospects: Limited certainly. Another drawback is that this creek, like several others in this district, dries up in hot seasons. It is not a good creek but there are fine colors here and there.

The Cle Elum river just upstream from Salmon La Sac. Fascinating and scenic country but generally poor placer ground.

Boulder Creek ● This is a tributary of famous Williams creek and runs into that stream from the east. Placer gold was first found on Boulder creek in 1891 by W. R. Hart. The ground upstream from its junction with Williams creek has yielded coarse gold with some nuggets topping the 10 ounce mark. The best ground is near the junction with the gravels becoming leaner upstream. Bedrock is deep in most parts of this creek and the gold is not as plentiful as it is on Williams.

Prospects: Because it was a poorer producer than other creeks close by, it was not mined as extensively. There is still some interesting looking ground along this stream. Difficulties getting to bedrock and water problems at depth. You might take a second look at this stream; it has possibilities.

A placer miner attempting to tap the deep ground on Boulder creek. The car is pulled up from the inclined shaft and the gold bearing gravel is dumped into a sluicebox. The Liberty region contains the richest placer gold creeks in Washington and their total production since the 1870s has been quite astonishing. The gold recovered has been legendary for its size. Boulder, however, is one of the leaner placer creeks in the area.

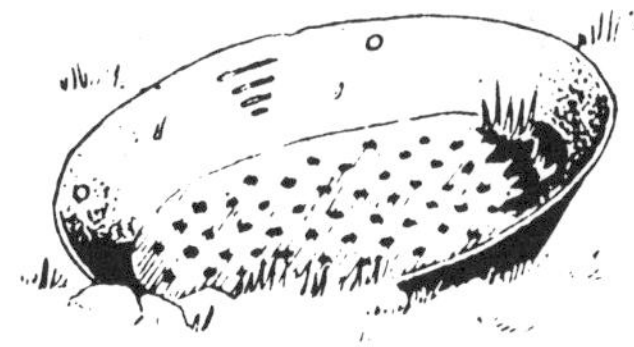

Cle-Elum River ● This placer river which runs into Cle-Elum Lake from the north has been sporadically mined for over a century. The gold is generally fine grained with occasionally coarser pieces from specific locations where the older and higher ancient channel cuts across the present river channel. Some of the bars, like Princeton Bar, yielded fairly well on occasion, especially during the early years. At other places like China Bend miners of the 1890s, like Ted Cooper, John Lind and Jimmy Wright sometimes took out over 20 ounces a season. The best stretch of this river is between its mouth and Fortune creek, with the coarsest gold close to the latter stream. The best gold is usually on bedrock although some bars have yielded relatively well from time to time. This river was mined by Chinese miners for years.

Prospects: Colors can be obtained at various places along the Cle-Elum but a continuous run does not seem to exist. Several prospectors have attempted to trace the purported high old channel on the eastern side of the river, but without much success. The Cle-Elum is generally considered to be a mediocre placer river best suited for recreational placer miners only.

Bedrock and boulders on the Cle-Elum river. Although this waterway has been mined off and on for over a hundred years, the results have been generally disappointing. The first Chinese miners obtained some gold at the mouths of creeks like Fortune and Salmon La Sac although it was usually fine. Some placer men contend that a high, ancient channel is on the eastern side of this river.

Fortune Creek ● This stream is the most productive tributary of the Cle-Elum. It flows into that river from the east and has yielded some of the coarsest placer gold in this particular area. The ground which yielded the majority of the gold was from its mouth upstream for just over ½ mile. Some of the original workings are still visible close to the creek on the north side below the canyon. A gang of Chinese miners mined Fortune creek for several seasons and took out significant but unrecorded amounts of gold. In 1895 two partners named Hicks and Jones worked the gravels near the mouth of Fortune creek, close to the old stamp mill site, with indifferent results.

Prospects: The flats on the north side of the creek have never been extensively prospected, especially the ground adjacent to the Chinese diggings. Like most of the branches of the Cle-Elum, however, Fortune creek is primarily a fine gold creek. It must be considered generally lean placer ground although there are some remote possibilities on the north side of this stream. Even in dry summers this creek maintains a consistent flow of water.

Tailings from the old Chinese miners who worked along Fortune Creek. Most of the Chinese workings are marked by neat rows of tailings and usually the site of the original Chinese camp is found close by. The old Chinese camp on Fortune, however, has not been located. The best ground is located on the north side of this stream, several hundred yards from its mouth.

Swauk Creek ● This is another illustrious placer creek in the Liberty district of Kittitas County. Discovered in 1868 when a deaf-mute named Bent Goodwin, camped by the stream with a prospecting party including his brother, found a ¾ ounce nugget. This discovery touched off a rush to the creek which was soon staked for several miles. The first miners on Swauk quickly discovered that it was bonanza ground, with nuggets ranging from an ounce to six ounces commonplace. Within a few years, that trinity of creeks; Swauk, Baker and Williams, were the three most famous placer gold producers in the state.

And Swauk continued to yield its golden harvest to placer miners like the Livingstone brothers, H. C. Jones, John Mayer and a host of others, including gangs of taciturn Chinese, who arduously tapped its riches. After the hand miners had gleaned the shallow gold deposits, the commercial dredges moved in. Their production was listed at about 4,200 ounces but, according to reliable local sources, the true total was probably 8,400 ounces because highgraders had helped themselves to much of the companies gold.

All in all, the total production of Swauk creek in more than one hundred and twenty years of mining has been estimated at not less than 45,000 ounces.

Some of the piles of tailings beside Swauk creek today. The commercial dredges mined somewhere between 4,200 and 8,400 troy ounces of gold.

An early print showing a mining camp in northwest Washington. This was typical of the scenes at the diggings in the early days - rough camp, tough miners.

Prospects: Swauk has an intriguing history but the best ground has been mined except for a few isolated and deep deposits. On the lower sections of this stream, several miles below the junction of Swauk and Williams, there is some fine gold which increases in fineness towards its union with the Yakima river. Surprisingly, some heavy nuggets lost during commercial dredging operations, still lie undetected under the dredge tailings piles close by the highway. Generally this creek has seen its best days. Unless you're willing to gamble on deep ground or take your chances on re-running old tailings, it might be wise to pass on this historic creek.

Early placer miners using a monitor in hydraulic mining somewhere in Washington. This was the most efficient method of placer mining. (photograph - Courtesy Eastern Washington State Historical Society)

Teanaway River ● This river rises in the Wenatchee Mountains and flows in a southeasterly direction to join the Yakima river just to the east of Cle Elum. There was some placer activity in the 1890s and a little in the 1930s on the Teanaway but it was never a good producer.

Prospects: Some very fine gold in isolated locations. This river is less than marginal. The total production was probably under 30 ounces of flour gold. Enjoy the river but don't count on much gold.

Williams Creek ● This is the finest gold creek in the state. Since its discovery in 1868, it has yielded, by conservative estimate, close to 80,500 ounces troy.

After Bent Goodwin's discovery on the Swauk in that year, it was only months before other prospectors began probing along its eastern tributary. The first major find made on Williams, about a mile above its mouth, was made by H. M. Cooper, an experienced prospector of the old school. Before long the stream was flooded with miners.

And those first years produced some of the coarsest gold nuggets ever found in Washington. Slugs of ¼ to ½ pound were seldom recorded because they were so commonplace. Other pieces ranged in weight from 17½ ounces to 28½ ounces and they were not unusual. By the 1890s, the miners discovered deep ground. Soon, deep shafts and tunnels drifting to bedrock were producing electrifying results. In this era, some of the most famous names in Williams creek history came to the fore. The "Big Three;" Tom Meagher, C. E. H. Bigney and Gus Nelson, all struck spectacular pay on their claims. Nelson recovering slightly more than 2,050 ounces from his ground near the forks, Tom Meagher recovered an astonishing 1,000 ounces and old man Bigney 1,120 ounces. At least an estimated 7,000 ounces was recovered in 1895 alone, by these three and half a dozen other big operators along the creek during that season.

An abandoned Northwest shovel standing in a field just below Liberty. This is one of numerous pieces of placer mining apparatus found close to famous Williams creek.

The majority of the gold on Williams was obtained from bedrock or from the gravels directly above that layer. And this creek, more than any other placer stream in Washington, continued to produce steadily, year after year. Much of the deep ground was in cemented gravels that made drifting on bedrock relatively safe and inexpensive.

There are many theories concerning the origin of the placer gold on Williams and nearby Swauk and Baker creeks. A cross-section of the nuggets reveals that the gold is compacted wire gold, lending credence to the theory that the gold originated close by.

Despite its extensive deep workings, Williams creek still holds great promise. The old timers got their share but the ancient channel which parallels and then crosses the more recent channel still has a significant amount of virgin ground, the gravels of which should give good results.

Prospects: All of the claims, even the marginal ones, are closely held and much of the ground is presently being mined. The chances are almost negligible that any ground will come up.

Yakima River ● This river flows southeasterly through the Yakima Valley before it joins the Columbia. Some fine gold was mined on the Yakima below the mouth of Swauk creek.

Prospects: The 1930s operation didn't yield much and the Yakima is not a noted placer river. Mainly isolated deposits of gravel with some flour gold just downstream from the Swauk creek entrance.

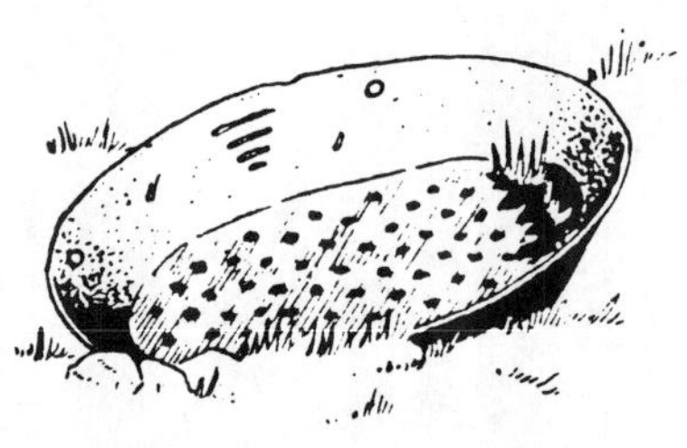

TREASURES & LOST MINES

Clarence Jordin Jr., the son of the famous mine-finder Clarence Jordin Sr. In the background is the old Virden cabin east of Liberty. Close by are the celebrated Ace of Diamonds, Gold King and Mountain Daisy mines.

THE GOLD VENT PUZZLE

"I guess the Jordins can smell gold," one of the old Liberty area miners once confided to me - and after lengthy research that surprising observation seems to be remarkably accurate. The first prospector in that noted family was George Jordin, who came into the Swauk - Liberty region in 1895; accompanied by six grandsons. Initially he tried his hand at placer mining, but his anticipated rewards were much less than he had anticipated, so he turned his energies and talents towards lode mining. Convinced, like others in the region, that the coarse gold in the creeks had originated from veins close at hand. He realized that the compressed gold recovered from Williams and the other streams in area was simply mashed lode gold and he, and several others set out to locate the motherlode, the source of all of the placer gold.

The initial lode discoveries in the immediate area had been made in 1887 when Thomas Tweed and William Johnson happened across a rich pocket of gold bearing quartz. Their find was so impressive that they built an arrastra to mill it and extracted some 900 ounces of gold from the quartz. This lode discovery spurred other prospectors into action and two years later George Hampton located the Red, a claim on a hill between Lyons and Kruger (now Cougar) gulches. In the summer of 1891,

A number of rich lode gold properties radiated out from Flag Mountain like the spokes of a wheel. For over a hundred years lode proppectors have been combing the nearby hills for the "Gold Vent."

Andy Flodin hit rich gold bearing bird's-eye quartz on his claim, the First of August. Other prospectors now began to shift slowly eastward as they fanned out in their ever widening search. Kruger Gulch suddenly came to the fore when in quick succession the Brown Bear Group, Bunker Hill, Dandy, Morning, the Livingstone Ledge, Bullion, Great Wonder and half a dozen other prospects and mines began yielding high grade ore to miners like Louis Quietsch, the Morrison brothers, Gus Nelson, Dr. O. M. Graves, Keith Dunlap, Evan Stander, Vestal Snyder and a handful of others.

In 1896, George Verdin discovered the Wall Street series, a ledge of narrow quartz veins carrying staggering amounts of free gold. This epic find, close to his placer workings on Boulder creek, resulted in his staking of two rich claims; the Badger and the Gold Vein. And both quickly became the talk of nearby Meaghersville. L. K. Hodges stated in 1897 that "George W. Verdin has taken some of the richest ore in camp from the two forks of the widest ledge of the Wall Street Series .... and several thousand dollars were cleaned up from one run of an arrastra."

This auspicious beginning not only launched the career of George Verdin but also focussed the search. George Jordin was now convinced, like Verdin, Flodin, Quietsch and others that there lay, somewhere in

The old Jordin cabin which still stands at the foot of Flag Mountain, close by the illustrious Gold King and Mountain Daisy mines.

the immediate area, a vast repository of gold ore of incalculable value, from which a network of rich quartz stringers were emanating. And this theory was passed on to his grandsons, five of whom would eventually follow in the footsteps of their grandfather.

By the turn of the century there were six or seven arrastras in the region east and northeast of Liberty. And the grandsons; Amos, Al, Henry, Ollie and Clarence, began to concentrate their prospecting in a rectangle measuring about ten miles by four miles, convinced that a treasure chest of immensely rich gold ore - the source of all of the placer gold - lay deep under the earth in this area. They prospected on Flag Mountain and on Nelson Hill and in Cougar Gulch. They meticulously combed every draw and hill in the region. Henry and Al prospected with limited success, Amos settled on a prospect on Nelson Hill and mined it for 54 years. But the last two, Ollie and Clarence, proved to be the ultimate prospectors, especially Clarence.

While prospecting around Flag Mountain, just east of old Liberty, Clarence staked an interesting prospect which he called the Gold King. Another prospector named Roy Mullins located the Mountain Daisy just to the south of the Gold King and abutting it on the same level. Roy Mullins, however, unable to find any veins of value, sold his "lemon" to Ollie Jordin in 1932. Working carefully the two Jordin brothers hit

The Jordin brothers prospected all through the rectangle to the north and east of Liberty, looking for the "Gold Vent."

spectacularly rich wire gold on both the Mountain Daisy and the Gold King. These electrifying discoveries became the talk of the camp, and in short order the two Jordin brothers became celebrities. During the next few years they mined thousands of ounces of wire gold, sometimes as much as several hundred ounces from a particularly rich pocket or vug. Ollie mined over 2,300 ounces from the Mountain Daisy during his ownership of the mine and Clarence produced even more gold out of the Gold King. Eventually both brothers sold their properties but stayed in Liberty to pursue the legendary "gold vent" which their grandfather had long believed existed somewhere east of Liberty.

Clarence Jordin, always considered the best prospector of the two brothers, painstakingly put together the clues. Most of the mines had been found between Boulder Creek and Nelson Hill and in that region - he was sure - lay other rich deposits. Finally, in 1946, he located a promising looking prospect that had been passed over by numerous fine prospectors. It was near Snowshoe Ridge and he called it the Ace of Diamonds. And what a find it was, surpassing even his wildest dreams. One pocket alone yielded 134 pounds of gold! Clarence and others were convinced that he had at last found the mythical "gold vent." The Ace of Diamonds was exceptionally rich, far more productive than any lode mine discovered up to that time in the area, but like the others, the

The remains of Clarence Jordin's Gold King mine. During its long and illustrious life it produced thousands of ounces of some of the finest wire gold ever to come out of the Liberty area.

pockets never developed into the continuous vein he was looking for. The Ace of Diamonds was Clarence Jordin's bonanza lode; estimates of the production from his workings in this mine usually credit him with a recovery of not less than 8,000 ounces with leasers later obtaining another 3,000 to 5,000 ounces.

Clarence Jordin passed away in 1965. By that time he was acknowledged as the premier lode prospector in the Liberty area and with two major discoveries to his credit his reputation was well deserved. But to the last Clarence Jordin insisted that the Ace of Diamonds, the Gold King, the Mountain Daisy and all of those other rich lode mines east of old Liberty were simply stringers radiating out from a "motherlode" which was deeply buried in that old rectangle.

Ollie Jordin continued the search until his death in the 1980s. And today there is another Jordin who has picked up the old quest of the family; his name is Clarence Benton Jordin Jr., a son of the famous mine-finder, who is a dedicated and persevering prospector in his own right. So Clarence Jr. takes up where his father and grandfather left off, equally convinced that somewhere in that ever fascinating region east of Liberty and maybe south as far as Kingfisher Mountain, a rich and massive "gold vent" lies waiting to be discovered. And who knows, the Jordin family may be right - they have been prospecting for that legendary lode for almost a hundred years.

Clarence Jordin in 1952 with about 150 ounces of wire gold. Clarence recovered several thousand ounces of gold during his career.

THE MISSING GOLD OF SWAUK CREEK

The estimates vary from $75,000.00 to well over $160,000.00 and probably the actual figure lies somewhere between those two figures. Swauk creek has long been acknowledged as one of the most productive placer streams in Washington and has produced prodigious quantities of the noble metal since its discovery in 1868. Much of the gold from that storied creek occurs in nugget form. And like most placer streams, the slugs found were seldom recorded. Swauk and the adjacent creeks, Baker and Williams, have yielded the largest nuggets in Washington. An idea of the coarseness of the Swauk creek gold may be obtained by examining the records of the creek in the 1890s. John Black, a long time Swauk creek miner recovered nuggets of 42 ounces, 23 ounces and 20 ounces, all in a single season. In 1887 the Livingstone brothers found three pieces; 29 ounces 14 pennyweight, 22 ounces and 14 ounces 17 pennyweight, as well as dozens of other nuggets weighing under half a pound troy. Swauk creek gold was unusually coarse.

By the 1920s, most of the shallow ground on the stream had been reasonably well mined, leaving only the bedrock on the deepest ground untouched. By the 1920s dredging companies began to move in. In 1922, the first dredge appeared on Swauk creek, but that dredge, owned by a company called the Swauk Mining & Dredging Company, proved to be too small to handle the boulders and the operation failed. In 1926 a much larger dredge, operated by the Kittitas Gold Mining Company, moved in to resume mining the deep gravels. Although this dredge recovered the

The 1926 dredge working the rich gravels of Swauk Creek. The various gold dredges recovered thousands of ounces of gold from Swauk.
(photograph - Courtesy Division of Geology and Earth Resources)

most gold, a recorded 2,100 ounces, but it also eventually abandoned the stream, citing various difficulties as the reasons. According to several local prospectors, however, the real reason was highgrading by the operators who allegedly stole several thousand ounces that should have gone into the company coffers. In 1940 one more attempt was made to tap the riches of Swauk. In that year the Clear Creek Dredging Co. produced over $50,000.00 after their dredge swept part of the stream. But that company was also plagued by theft and shut down after the end of the season.

All three companies had not only lost considerable amounts of gold to highgraders, but they had also made another very costly mistake, a miscalculation common to most operators of large dredges. Their gravel screens were designed to take all material under ¾". This meant that every nugget larger than ¾" rolled off the screens onto the tailings piles. The owners had not made provision for the huge nuggets found on Swauk creek and every one of those nuggets had ended up on the waste dumps by the side of the creek.

Eventually this error came to light during the 1950s when a woman picked up a beautiful 16 ounce nugget almost at the top of one of the numerous tailings piles. Over the next few years approximately twenty to thirty more huge slugs were found by more systematic searchers who used metal detectors.

As even the most sophisticated detectors are only effective to a relatively shallow depth, they usually do not detect discarded nuggets that are deeply buried in a tailings pile. It stands to reason that the vast majority of these nuggets that slipped past the dredge screens are still exactly where they were dropped those many years ago.

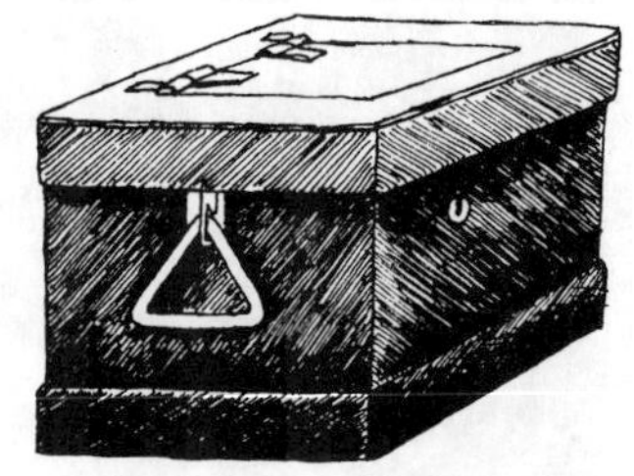

Although the official production from the three dredging operations yielded slightly over 2,400 ounces of gold, it is probable that the dredge crews highgraded at least an equal amount; placing the true production at somewhere around 8,400 troy ounces.

Assuming that only 3% to 4% of the gold passing through was over ¾", not a high estimate considering the reputation of Swauk creek, a total of somewhere between 252 and 336 ounces ended up on the tailings piles. With gold valued at an estimated $475 per troy ounce, the buried nuggets are worth anywhere from $120,000 to $160,000, and perhaps more, because most of them are specimen pieces which always bring more than the spot price.

The missing gold of Swauk creek still lies under those old dredge tailings close by today's highway. Sometime, someone will run all of those old tailings through a plant - and then the puzzle of the buried gold of Swauk creek will finally be resolved.

PLACER GOLD PARTICULARS

A monitor in a hydraulic pit in the northern goldfields.

This section outlines some of the particulars and indicators that knowledgeable placer miners should be aware of. It also includes a short glossary of placer mining words and terms.

PLACER GOLD LOCATIONS IN NORTH EASTERN WASHINGTON

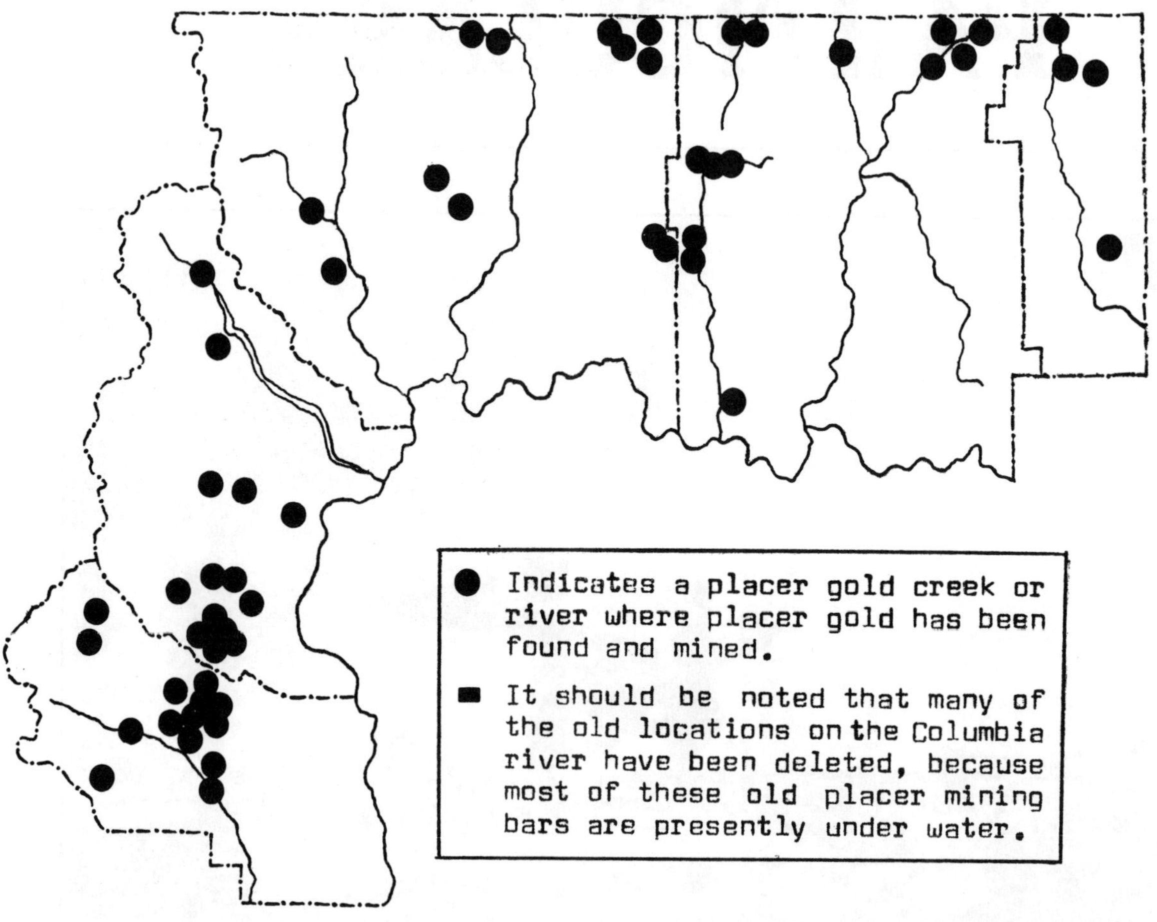

The various locations indicated on the accompanying map have been provided by the Division of Geology and Earth Resources, Olympia, Washington. Other locations have been obtained from information provided by placer miners from Kittitas, Chelan, Okanogan, Ferry, Stevens and Pend Oreille counties, and from personal observation, field trips and testing.

Kittitas, Chelan and Okanogan counties are considered by most placer men to be the most productive areas in the six counties indicated on the map above. Kittitas, especially close to the Liberty area, has produced the majority of the gold as well as the coarsest gold.

GLOSSARY

ALLOY • A mixture of two or more metals. An alloy is usually made for a specific reason; such as to harden a metal or occasionally to debase a valuable metal such as gold with a less valuable metal like copper, without altering the appearance of the richer metal.

ASSAY • An analysis of an ore or metal to determine the proportion, or the purity of its ingredients. Thus, if a sample of ore assays high in gold, it contains a relatively high proportion of gold in comparison to other metals or components.

BAR • This is a projection of sand or gravel into a stream or river. The bars of certain rivers like the Columbia, Similkameen, Pend Oreille and Kettle, were often or sometimes gold bearing. Usually the gold is fine grained although some bars, like famous Rich Bar of Similkameen fame, were prodigious producers of gold.

BEDROCK • This is the most important term is placer mining. Bedrock is the impervious layer of rock underlying a watercourse, to which placer gold gravitates and settles. The gold usually finds its way into cracks or crevices or under boulders on bedrock and collects there. About 95% of all placer gold is found on bedrock and this layer must be carefully cleaned by the miner.

BLACK SAND • This fine grained material usually occurs with placer gold and may make up most of the concentrates in the pan. Black sand is often magnetite and can be removed from the gold pan after drying by using a magnet. Black sand is an indicator of gold and if it is not present in the gravels being tested, it is unlikely that gold exists in that spot.

BULLION • Usually an ingot of metal, often gold or silver, which has been refined by melting down the crude metal and removing the impurities.

CHINA DIGGINGS • This phrase originated in the goldfields of California, and was carried north into Washington by argonauts from that state. It It was used to describe placer ground which was being mined by Chinese miners and considered poor by white standards. It was later discovered that some of the "Chinese Diggings" were far richer than had previously been suspected, a fact which the shrewd and taciturn Chinese had wisely kept from the white miners.

CLAIM JUMPING • Along with sluice-box robbery, this was considered one of the most serious crimes in the mining camps of the early west. This phrase probably originated in California and soon gained common usage throughout the west. Claim jumping was the act of illegally restaking a claim which had been legally staked by another miner. Often a bloody and sometimes deadly affray occurred over disputes arising from "claim jumping." In the early court records in Kittitas, Chelan, Pend Oreille and Okanogan counties there are numerous references to vicious fights, shootings and even murder as a direct result of this offence.

CLEAN-UP This is the term used to describe the procedure of recovering gold after the gold bearing gravels have been washed. Various types of sluices were used during the washing of the gravels and the clean-up entails the careful cleaning of riffles, apron or any other apparatus used to catch or trap gold. This is the final step in placer mining.

COLORS This is the term used to describe particles of gold, sometimes only flakes or mere specks. "colors" in the pan, sluicebox or rocker are indicative of gold bearing ground. The more numerous and heavier the colors, the more promising the area. Good placer men have always, and still do keep a sharp lookout for this indicator.

CONCENTRATES This is accumulated material remaining in the pan or in the sluicebox after washing, the majority of this residue is commonly called blacksand, although the concentrates may also include platinum, native silver, copper, electrum, ironstone or some other heavier wash. The residue is then carefully separated - and the methods of separation are many and varied - and the gold and other precious metals are saved.

DEAD WORK This is a phrase used by placer men to describe the labor of driving toward paydirt. Dead work was usually expensive and unrewarding, especially when the overburden was deep. It almost always involved the removal of barren gravel before the pay was reached.

DRIFTING This simply means horizontal tunneling into a bank in order to reach paydirt on bedrock or to follow a promising lead. Shallow and easily worked pay gravels were usually rapidly exhausted and after that drifting was resorted to, but only if the paydirt was considered rich enough to warrant the expense.

FINENESS This word expresses the relative purity of placer gold, in other words, the ratio of gold to silver in placer gold. The gold from each locality in the state varies considerably in fineness. If the gold from a specific creek or river assays .878 fine, that means that gold has 878 parts gold out of 1000. Placer gold is, of course, never pure, hence the difference in price from district to district.

FOOL'S GOLD This is miner's jargon for any material which looks like, or resembles gold and is taken for the real thing by the inexperienced. The most common substance mistaken for gold is mica. Mica is found in many placer creeks but its properties are considerably different than gold; it is much lighter, tends to float in the pan, splits easily upon handling and does not reflect light when in shadow. Iron pyrites can be misleading as well but they are usually cubical and angular. Both mica and pyrites, when visually compared with gold, are easily identified.

GRIZZLY A screen or some other device used to keep boulders or rocks out of the sluice-box. A grizzly is usually set over or near the head of a sluice at an angle so that all oversize material will roll off.

GROUND SLUICING The use of water to wash away overburden to reach the bedrock. Sometimes called "booming".

HARDPAN This is a false bedrock, invariably a hard clay layer. Gold was often found lying on this layer and in those instances it acted like a true bedrock. Often, however, gold penetrated this layer and came to rest on bedrock. Sometimes gold is on both layers.

HIGHGRADING This is the domain of unscrupulous wretches. It is the act of the unprincipled in stealing gold from another miner's sluicebox; the theft of gold from a trusting partner or associate or cheating in the cleanup. Unfortunately, a relatively high percentage of placer men fall into this category. In the old west the penalties ranged from expulsion from the district, jail, and occasionally, the death penalty.

HYDRAULIC This is a word used to describe a common method of mining in which water under pressure is utilized to cut away banks of gold-bearing gravels or overburden. Water is brought into an operation by pipes or flumes; high enough above the operation to provide a "head." The water is then discharged into a pipeline, which has a large mounted nozzle, called a "monitor" or a "giant." By carefully directing the stream of water under pressure, the overburden was cut away and the gold-bearing gravels exposed and sluiced, using the water provided.

JOHN A derogatory term used to designate a Chinese miner. This word originated in California in the 1850s and was carried northward by the miners from the Golden State. Fortunately, this word is no longer used.

KARAT This word is used to describe the purity of refined gold. Thus, 24 karats is pure gold, 20 karats is 20/24ths pure. The letters 10K on a piece of jewellery would indicate that the item was only 10/24ths pure with the remainder consisting of a silver or copper alloy.

LEAD This word has two meanings. It is sometimes used to describe a "run" of gold which occurs on nearly all placer streams. It is usually the layer upon which the highest values are encountered. "Lost leads" are runs which cannot be traced or followed by placer miners. It also means extremely coarse gold. "Lead gold" is uniformly heavy and nuggety gold which probably came from an ancient rich channel.

LODE This word is used to describe the place of origin of the metal being mined. Hence the lode is the starting place of the metal. It was often searched for by prospectors who anticipated finding the "metal in place." The "motherlode" is the main place of origin of the metal.

MERCURY Often referred to as "quick" or "quicksilver" by placer men, and was used by them to recover fine gold from the blacksand because of the peculiar affinity of mercury to amalgamate or combine with the gold. Later, the gold in the resulting "amalgam" was recovered by driving off the mercury by retorting, this can be extremely hazardous and novices should not attempt it. Leave the handling of mercury to the experts.

NUGGET A word meaning a lump, piece or specimen of native gold. This word was probably derived from "nug," an old English word which meant "lump." It is generally used to describe any piece of gold which weighs 1 grain or more.

OVERBURDEN This is ground which must be penetrated or removed in order to reach the paygravels on bedrock. Usually the overburden consists of barren or poor paying gravels.

PLACER These are deposits of sand or gravel which contain particles of gold or other valuable heavy minerals. Gold was, and still is, the most important mineral found in placers. This word was probably derived from a Spanish word meaning "sand bank."

POKE A small leather bag used by prospectors in the early years to store and carry their placer gold. It is usually about 6 inches in length and 2 inches in width, with a draw-string at the top. Used only occasionally today, it has been largely replaced by less romantic containers made of plastic or metal.

POT-HOLE A word used to describe a depression in the bed-rock of a stream. Highly over-rated as they seldom contain appreciable amounts of gold because any gold which has been deposited in them is ground fine by the action of water and gravel after which the fine gold washes out.

SNIPING This is the practice of a miner re-working old ground which has been mined previously. This may entail re-working old tailings, especially in areas where cemented gravels were present, a condition which made the recovery of gold in the early days difficult. Other snipers concentrate solely on working crevices in bedrock.

STAKE This word has a dual meaning. It may mean the action of placing tags on a claimpost in order to legally hold mining ground. It is also used to describe occasions when a miner is able to amass placer gold in such quantity that he is able to retire, either temporarily or permanently from mining. Thus the phrase "making a stake" implies that a prospector has made enough money from mining that he is financially independent, a condition which, unfortunately, seldom lasted long.

TAILINGS This is a specialized term used to describe the residue left over after a mining operation. In placer mining, the larger boulders and rocks, discarded and often piled or left along the banks of gold creeks, are referred to as "tailings."

TROY WEIGHT In calculating the weight of gold and silver, a different scale called "Troy weight" is used. The word "Troy" was probably derived from the name of an ancient French town called Troyes, where a celebrated fair was held during the 16th century. Troy weight is figured differently than the usual avoirdupois weight, which is the common standard used in calculating the weight of articles other than gold and silver. A comparison of the two scales is given below:

TROY WEIGHTS

24 grains	1 pennyweight
480 grains	20 pennyweights
20 pennyweights	1 Troy ounce
5760 grains	12 Troy ounces
12 Troy ounces	1 Troy pound

AVOIRDUPOIS WEIGHTS

437½ grains	1 ounce
7000 grains	16 ounces
16 ounces	1 pound

WING-DAM A type of dam built into the bed of a gold-bearing stream or river in order to be able to mine the bedrock. The Chinese were skilled wing-dammers. Although this method of recovering gold is rarely used now, it was a favourite way of mining in the 19th century.

1. <u>BEDROCK</u> ● Undoubtedly the most important term in placer mining. Approximately 94% of all placer gold is located on this impervious layer of rock, or in its cracks and crevices. Gold, being an extremely heavy metal, gradually works down through the gravels and eventually comes to rest on the bedrock. Experienced placer miners always work to bedrock where most of the gold lies.

2. <u>HARDPAN or FALSE BEDROCK</u> ● This is a hard layer of clay which acts somewhat like a true bedrock and sometimes holds gold. Occasionally gold will be found on both the false bedrock and on true bedrock.

3. <u>EXITS and ENTRANCES of CANYONS</u> ● The old-time prospectors always prospected entrances and exits to canyons realizing that both before and after the narrow constriction of a canyon that the current slows, allowing the gold to settle. Exits are generally more productive than entrances. Another peculiarity is that there are often multiple runs of gold in the gravels directly below the exit of a canyon.

4. <u>THE BLUE LEAD</u> ● Sometimes called "The California Lead," this is a grayish-blue layer often found directly above a rich pre-glacial or tertiary channel. Early prospectors watched carefully for this layer which often indicated that exceptionally rich placer ground lay directly beneath it.

5. <u>FLAT WASH</u> ● Another excellent sign of good ground. Flat wash is the term used to describe flat rocks or flat boulders which are found in gravel. Often gravel with flat wash in it was bonanza ground.

6. <u>BLACKSAND and IRONSTONE</u> ● Both of these are made up of hematite or magnetite particles. Because they are heavy in iron, they tend to be found where gold is found. The concentrates are largely made up of blacksand and some ironstone.

7. <u>COLORS</u> ● One of the age-old signs for a good placer man. Colors are minute particles of gold, indicators that gold is present in the gravels. Unfortunately, some colors are so small that they are almost microscopic so colors are best judged by weight and not by numbers.

8. <u>CEMENTED GRAVELS</u> ● Quite often cemented gravels carry a higher percentage of gold than ordinary gravels. Always check occurences of cemented gravels when in a placer gold locality.

9. <u>OXIDIZED GRAVELS</u> ● Again a fine indicator. Usually the oxidized gravels are coppery colored and sometimes partially cemented. A good placer prospector always checks out oxidized gravels, especially when they lie directly above the bedrock.

10. <u>ANCIENT CHANNELS</u> ● The great placer discoveries of the future will be the old or tertiary channels. Sometimes these hidden channels are located on low benches close to present watercourses, whereas at other times they may lie far above, sometimes hundreds of feet above todays waterways. A significant number of these ancient channels are spectacularly rich, however, experienced placer prospectors are the most successful in locating these old channels, amateur placer miners seldom find them.

11. HISTORIC PLACER REGIONS ● Always prospect in or close to the old proven placer areas. The old-time placer miners probably prospected or mined virtually every creek and river in Washington and discovered the gold bearing watercourses. Historic regions like the Liberty region in Kittitas County, the Peshastin area in Chelan County, the region south of and close by Republic in Ferry County, the Okanogan Highlands and the Western Okanogan in Okanogan County and the Sullivan Creek district in Pend Oreille County are probably the best bets in the six counties. The chances of discovering a virgin placer gold creek are slim indeed. The best gold creeks have already been found so stay in the old regions.

12. PROSPECT BELOW 5,000' ELEVATION ● Few placer creeks lie above the 5,000' level, so it would be wise to restrict your prospecting to those streams which lie below that elevation, at least in Washington. Most of the placer gold originated locally and as there is little weathering or erosion above that level, there is little placer gold to be found.

13. INSIDE BENDS ● It is well known that inside bends, places where the current slackens, collect fine gold.

14. GEOLOGICAL ABNORMALITIES ● Old hands in placer mining are always keeping an eye out for geological oddities. Some things to look for are changes in the color of gravel, abrupt changes in the type of bedrock, the discovery of large contoured boulders, concentrations of ironstone or a preponderance of garnets. Abnormalities often occur and indicate El Dorado ground.

15. DOWNSIDE of BOULDERS ● Experienced placer miners always work the downriver side of boulders because the back eddy which forms there is a collecting basin for placer gold. Placer gold is seldom found on the upriver side of the rock.

16. BEYOND OLD WORKINGS and OVERLOOKED GROUND ● The price of a troy ounce of placer gold in the early days generally ran somewhere between $15 and $16 an ounce. If the ground failed to pay wages, it was usually abandoned. Today, with gold at approximately thirty times the 1860s to 1920s price, that same ground may well be worth looking at. It is also good practice to examine old ground to see if the original gold miners overlooked ground. Nearly all of the old cabin sites are still standing on virgin, unworked ground. The old-timers didn't build their cabins on tailings because they couldn't set their base logs correctly, so they built on unmined ground, ground that is still there today.

17. ACCUMULATION of BOULDERS or BOULDER NESTS ● Buildups of boulders usually occur some distance downstream from waterfalls. Waterfalls, of course, are poor places to prospect because the turbulence at the foot of the falls which smoothes out the bedrock there and carries the gold downstream. Boulders tend to accumulate some distance from waterfalls, and prospecting should begin there.

18. DIAGONAL CREVICES and STEPPING BEDROCK ● Contrary to the general belief, diagonal crevices tend to hold more gold than horizontal ones.

Horizontal crevices, although ideally placed in relation to the current, are inclined to pack with gravel, causing the gold to pass over them, whereas diagonal crevices which face upriver into the current usually catch passing gold and are self-cleaning of gravels. Stepping bedrock is the name given to bedrock that slopes gently into a creek or river. It's the kind of bedrock that is usually easy to mine because bedrock is usually shallow.

19. FLOOD GOLD ● Highly overrated. Generally only small amounts of placer gold is carried downriver during the spring runoff or floods. Some of the major rivers do deposit a certain amount of fine gold in the spring, enabling bar miners to recover gold on specific bars each season. Generally only the top few inches of gravel on the bar carry gold.

20. JUNCTIONS of CREEKS and RIVERS ● All experienced placer miners are aware that the junctions of waterways are promising locations to prospect. The reason for this is that there is often a secondary or double enrichment at the junction, primarily because placer gold may be coming from two sources, from the river and from the tributary.

21. SEVEN FOOT and OTHER SHALLOW GROUND ● Old placer men watch for seven foot and other shallow ground. Today seven foot ground may be productive because it was passed up by the original Chinese miners. They realized that seven feet to bedrock was too deep, because they couldn't shovel gravel up to that height. Chinese miners, logical to a fault, routinely walked away from shallow ground when it required tunneling which was an expensive proposition.

22. LEAD GOLD ● This is the term used to describe extremely coarse placer gold. Historically this type of gold marks an old channel and when placer miners encountered "lead" gold, they knew that an ancient, rich channel was close at hand. This is an important indicator.

TREASURE TROVE INFORMATION

The few treasure items pictured above are a minute part of the more than $142,000.00 in treasure recovered by the author over the past two decades of wandering through the West. The treasure consists of gold and silver coins, placer gold and platinum, raw silver and bar silver, jewellery and other valuable items. Almost all of the finds were made in historic mining regions or in ghost towns.

This section is devoted to the various indicators and signs that the professional treasure hunters look for. Indeed the hints may make the difference between locating a cache or passing it by.

Although many treasures and caches have been found in the state in the last two decades, most of them have been located in one of the old mining counties. And it is generally conceded that a tiny handful of experienced and knowledgeable treasure hunters have unearthed more treasures than all of the many thousands of amateurs combined. There are many reasons for this disparity.

Generally the successes of the professionals can be attributed to research, perseverance, observation and luck. Of those, certainly the most important factor is research.

Although these are literally hundreds of treasure stories in circulation in Washington; the majority of these tales are simply grossly exaggerated or non-existant. Out of every one hundred treasure tales research indicates that an average of close to seven stories are worth following up. It should be emphasized, however, that not every historic treasure tale should be discarded out-of-hand. If a certain story has circulated for years in an area and has hard details; dates, general location, names, place names and other specific evidence, it is wise to check it out. If, however, there are no hard facts and only vague generalities, it is most likely a bar-room tale and it should be dismissed as such.

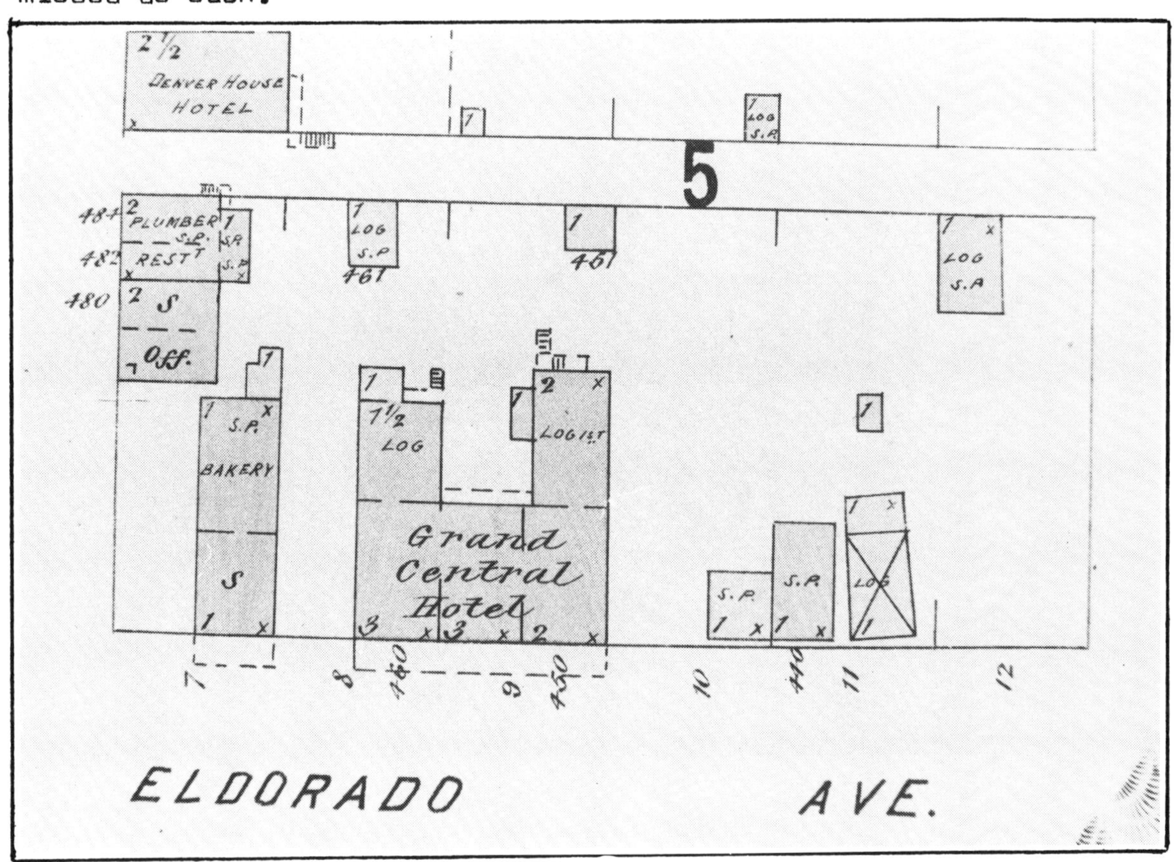

Fire insurance company maps such as this reveal little known but often important details ; the location and length of boardwalks, the exact size and type of building, the position of entrances, the width of the streets and so on. This information, of course, is invaluable for the researcher interested in historic towns.

The remote mining regions are usually the most productive of all areas for treasure hunters to explore. There are a number of reasons for this statement, which I will ennumerate. Firstly, the majority of the old mining camps were established in remote areas where there were no banks. Secondly, few miners or prospectors trusted either banks or paper currency because many of the early banks had bankrupted and had left their depositors high, dry and broke - and holding only worthless paper notes. Consequently, most of these men tended to be "hard metal" men, believing only in the pure metals; gold and silver, and trusting solely to their own devices to safeguard their hard won earnings. And they chose a bewildering number of places to secret their money. Some selected the obvious hiding places; basements or cellars, under loose floor boards, in mattresses, behind walls, behind loose or removeable stones in fireplaces or chimneys, in attics or in some other generally simple hiding place. Others were more imaginative, selecting a piece of furniture such as a desk with a hidden drawer or some other hollow receptacle, or cached in the gloomy recesses of a root cellar. Others were genuinely inspired, using both logic and imagination. In 1970, a treasure hunter from Seattle found an oak nail keg filled to the brim with gold and silver coins in an abandoned mine tunnel, nearly 90 feet

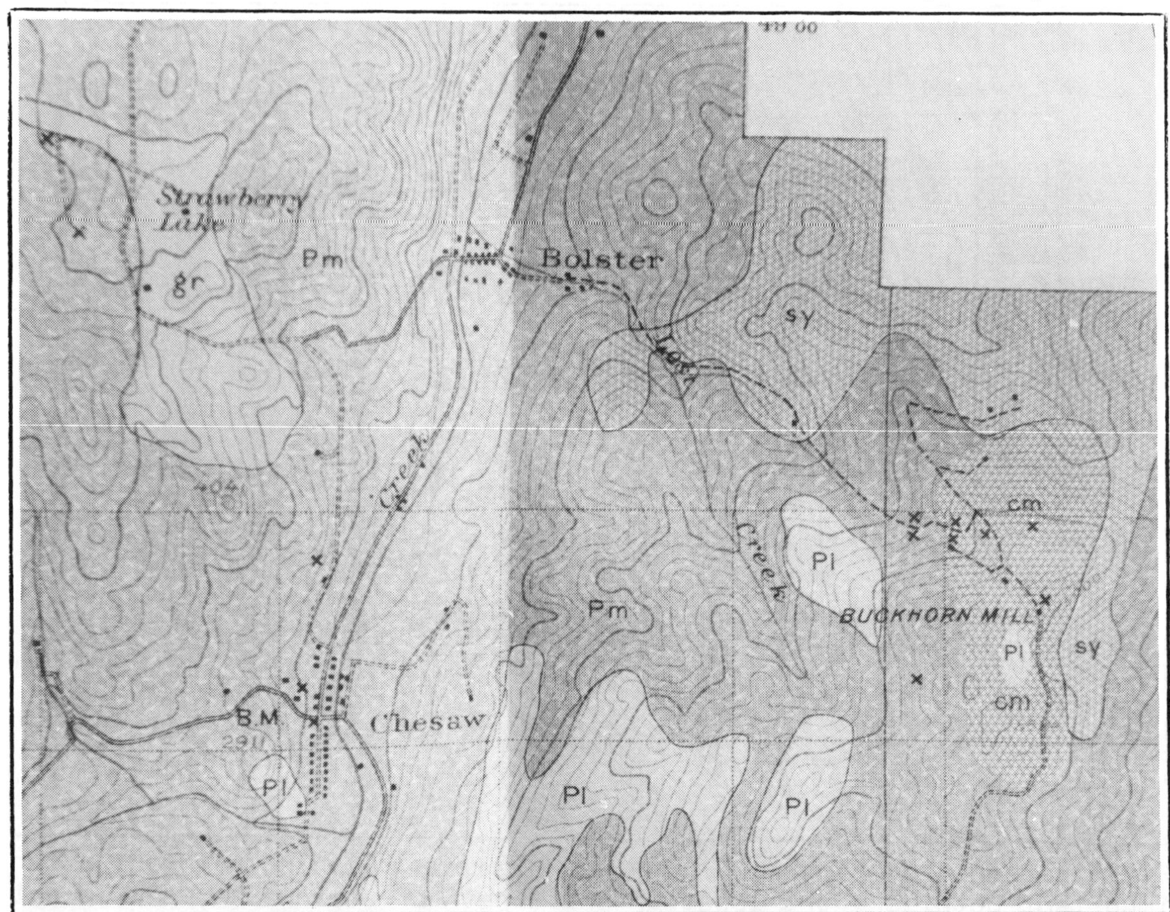

Detail of a map from Bulletin No. 5 of the 1911 Washington Geological Report shows the Chesaw-Bolster area of Okanogan County; some mineral prospects and mines and 92 buildings which were standing in that year.

GHOST TOWNS, MINING TOWNS, LOST MINE & TREASURE LOCATIONS IN NORTH EASTERN WASHINGTON

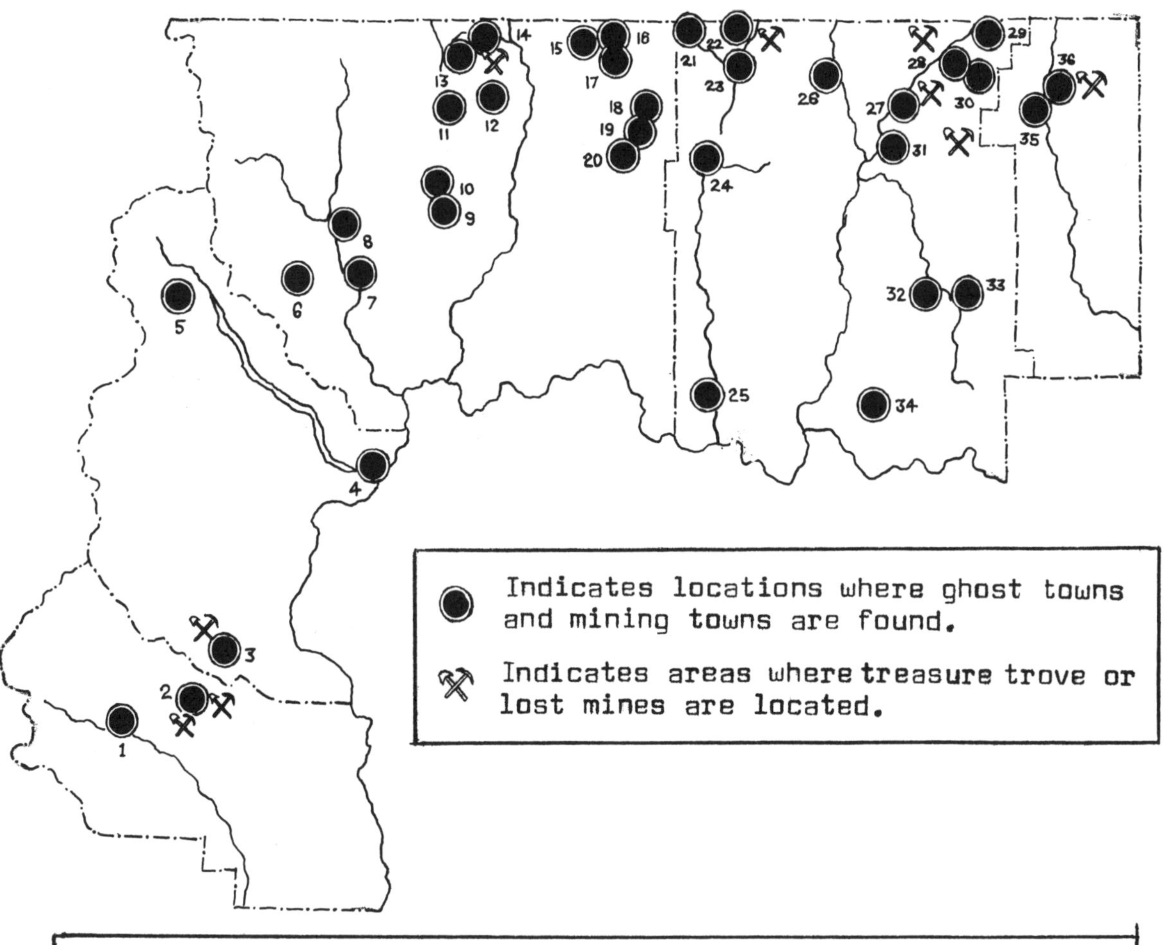

1 Roslyn
2 Liberty
3 Old Blewett
4 Chelan
5 Holden
6 Gilbert
7 Twisp
8 Winthrop
9 Ruby
10 Conconully
11 Loomis
12 Golden
13 Nighthawk
14 Okanogan City
15 Molson
16 Bolster
17 Chesaw
18 Bodie
19 Old Toroda
20 Wauconda
21 Ferry
22 Danville
23 Curlew
24 Republic
25 Keller
26 Orient
27 Bossburg
28 Northport
29 Boundary
30 Leadpoint
31 Marcus
32 Addy
33 Chewelah
34 Cedarville
35 Ione
36 Metaline Falls

from its entrance. This spectacular find was worth nearly $148,000.00 to its fortunate discoverer. The treasure had lain undisturbed in its original hiding place since 1898, the date when its unlucky owner had died in a cave-in. The old miner had been working alone on a bonanza vein when he was killed. Eventually his body was found, he was buried and eventually forgotten. Nobody was aware that he had converted all of his substantial profits from his mine into gold and silver specie, most of that in $20 and $10 gold pieces; double eagles and eagles. He had his own bank, like so many miners, depositing only gold and silver coins into it, until his tragic accident. The nail keg simply stayed where he had left it, on top of the timbering and in total darkness - completely out of sight until it was discovered in 1970, some 72 years later. The discoverer neglected to inform the IRS of his amazing find and although there were (and are) witnesses, the precise details and the names of the individuals involved remain on file because of legal complications and will remain in that status until the principals are deceased. Two other major treasure trove discoveries, valued at nearly $220,000.00 and $372,000.00 respectively, also fall into the category of unreported treasures. The first one, located in 1972, consisted of twelve cigar boxes full of gold coins, the second totalled just over

Gold double eagles and eagles, like the coins shown above, were found accidently by a carpenter in 1972 in the basement of an old house in a famous mining town. The coins were worth $220,000.00.

900 old gold coins, all of the same denomination, which were found in 1979 in a small iron-bound wooden strongbox which was lying under the floorboards of a recluse's abandoned shack. Each of these treasures, which have been carefully documented, were stumbled across, not found as the result of dedicated research on the part of the discoverer. It goes without saying that there have been hundreds of treasure troves found in the past twenty years that have not been reported. It is also reasonable to assume that there are many hundreds of treasures which still await discovery in Washington.

An intelligent treasure seeker should carefully evaluate all of the information available, determine whether the hoard has been found but not reported and finally calculate the chances of success. If the reputed treasure meets enough of the necessary criteria, an expedition should be undertaken.

For some reason old Chinese diggings have generally been poorly searched. It is well known that the Oriental miners were the finest of all placer men although their avarice was legendary. Old Chinese camps in the placer gold fields are almost always marked by straight rows of boulders or tailings and usually close to the diggings are the remains of one or more Chinese habitations. These should be carefully checked

Some articles found by the author at an old Chinese store site close to some Chinese placer workings. Pictured are several delicate silver ornaments, a 24K gold pin, some mixed coins, some musket balls and an assortment of other items recovered from the site by screening.

as they sometimes contain valuable items. A number of gold, silver and jade artifacts, as well as more commonplace copper and brass articles have been recovered in a few of the sites. Many old Chinese diggings are located along the upper part of the Columbia River, from about 10 miles west of Northport and on upriver to the border, this section of that magnificent river still flows almost unimpeded since the Chinese argonauts toiled along its bars and benches so many years ago. Other Chinese mining sites are located throughout the six counties, usually close to historic placer gold creeks.

Both Chinese and white miners, it should be noted, usually mined either placer gold or free gold from quartz veins, both of which were easily turned into cash when the need arose. In some cases, however, that particular requirement never came up. So, many miners, often old and reclusive, spent only what was necessary for daily living and then concealed the remainder of their gold in a hiding place in their cabins or somewhere else close by - a hoard for a rainy day. In a surprising number of cases these caches remained exactly where they were hidden by their owners - and remain there to this day.

Chinese gold scales in bamboo carrying case, several hundred Chinese brass coins in the original canvas bag and a brass blowing pan which was used by Chinese placer miners during the 1860s. The items shown in the photograph are only a few of the hundreds of Chinese artifacts recovered in or near the historic Chinese camps scattered throughout Washington.

LODE GOLD & SILVER LOCATIONS IN NORTH EASTERN WASHINGTON

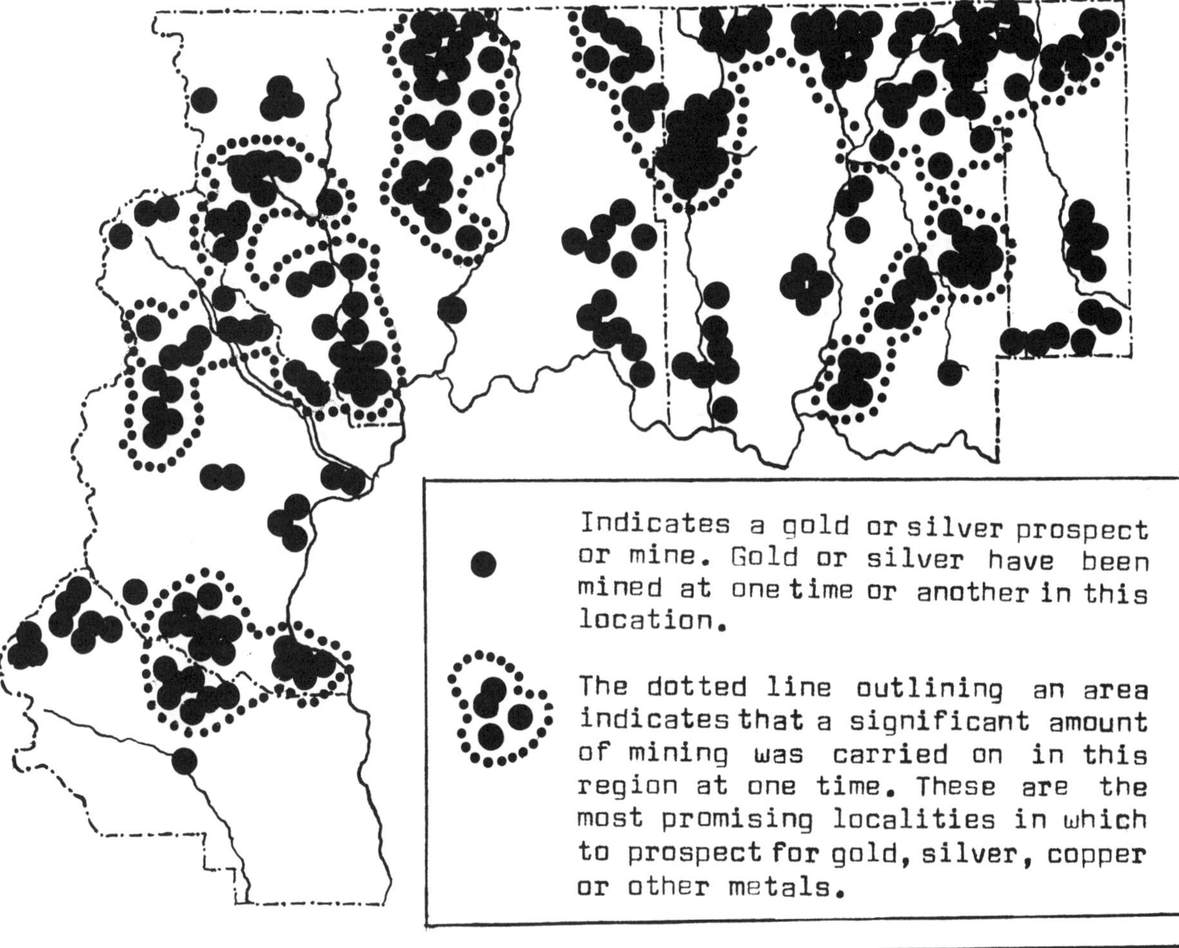

The lode gold and silver locations indicated on the accompanying map have been provided from information obtained from the Division of Geology and Earth Resources, Olympia, Washington. Other data and information have been drawn from Bulletin No. 69, "Silver Occurrences of Washington," by Wayne S. Moen and from Information Circular 57, "Handbook for Gold Prospectors in Washington," by W. S. Moen and Marshall T. Huntting. Details from Bulletins 6, 10, 2 and other publications from the Division were also useful. The additional information was provided by numerous old miners from the six counties and from personal observations, files, notes and field trips into the locations.

On the other hand, the chances of locating a long lost mine are not nearly as limited as expected, especially when compared to finding a major lost treasure. Over the decades, in the six mining counties covered in this book, many thousands of prospects have been discovered and hundreds of mines have come into production, a surprising number of them high grade properties.

Although uncounted numbers of dedicated and relentless prospectors have combed the mining country for a century or more, there are many hundreds, and perhaps thousands, of high grade deposits still awaiting discovery in the old mining regions. On the surface this may seem like an exaggeration but the evidence suggests otherwise and supports this claim.

Each year major mining companies return to the mining districts in a continuing effort to locate previously missed ore deposits. These companies realize that prospecting is at best an imperfect science and because nearly 91% of the terrain is covered by overburden, they know that most of the ore deposits remain undetected. This point is illustrated when one considers one of the classic cases in the mining annals of the state. Clarence Jordin of Liberty, in Kittitas County, was one

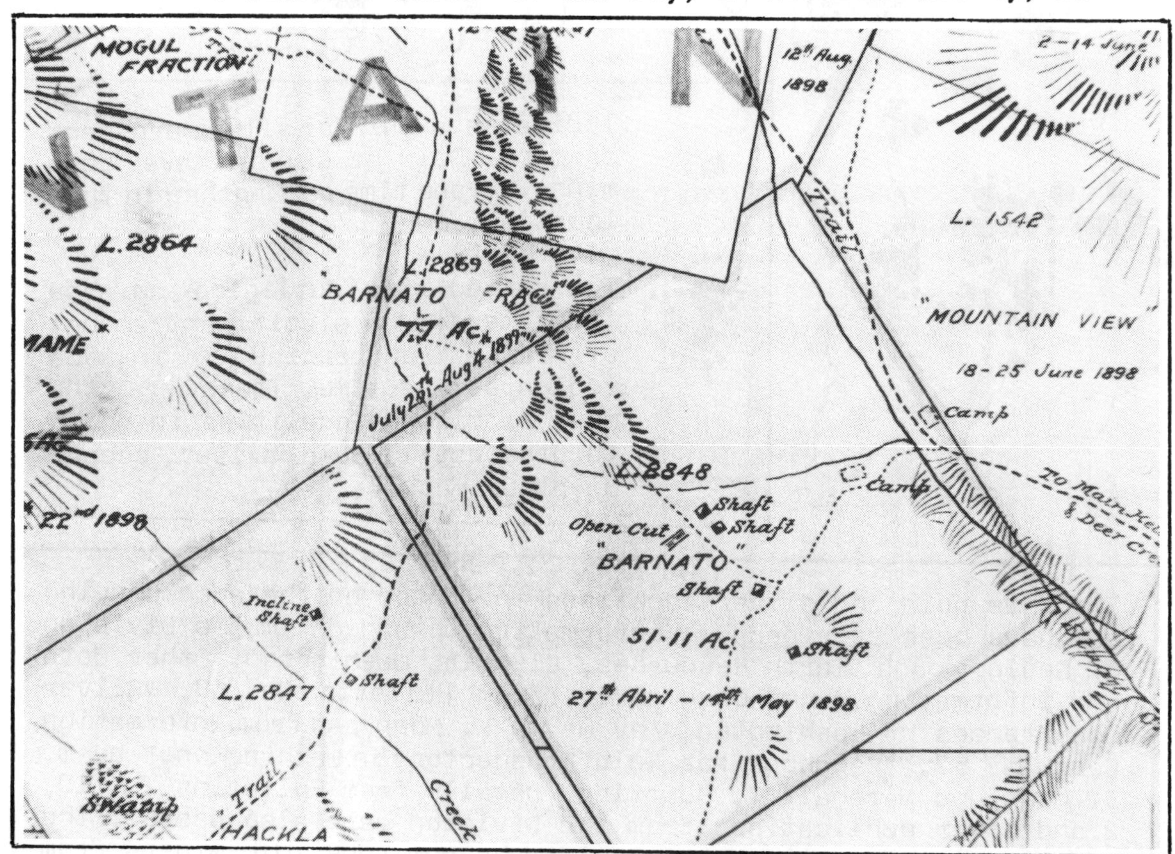

Details of this 1903 mining map show cabins, shafts, tunnels and other data of significance. In many areas the original cabins have vanished, victims of time, fire, vandalism or the Forest Service, and maps such as this one are an important record, especially if the mining camp was short-lived and relatively obscure.

of the finest hardrock prospectors in the county. In 1928 he found the rich Gold King Mine at the base of Flag Mountain, barely five hundred yards east of the old placer camp of Liberty. While he was mining the Gold King, convinced that an extension of the mineralized zone lay in the immediate vicinity he began searching for it. In 1952, twenty-four years later, he finally found it and staked the Ace of Diamonds claim on Snowshoe Ridge, just north and east of the Gold King, it proved to be one of the most spectacular finds in Kittitas County. The Clarence Jordin story is covered in detail in the Kittitas County section but this case illustrates the difficulties encountered even by experienced prospectors who know their district intimately. There are innumerable other and similar instances in the state and all serve to bear out the statement that "Many mines remain to be found."

Certainly serious treasure and lost mine enthusiasts are advised to concentrate on the following regions:

1. The Nighthawk-Loomis Area of Okanogan County
2. The Golden-Conconully Area of Okanogan County
3. The Twisp-Winthrop-Mazama Area of Okanogan County
4. The Old Toroda-Bodie Area of Okanogan County
5. The Republic Area of Ferry County
6. The Curlew-Danville Area of Ferry County
7. The Orient Area of Ferry County
8. The Northport-North Columbia Area of Stevens County
9. The Leadpoint Area of Stevens County
10. The Deep Creek Area of Stevens County
11. The Queen of Sheba-Uncle Sam Mtn. Area of Stevens County
12. The Metaline Falls-Sullivan Creek Area of Pend Oreille County
13. The Holden Area of Chelan County
14. The Wenatchee Area of Chelan County
15. The Blewett Pass Area of Chelan County
16. The Liberty-Swauk Creek Area of Kittitas County

The sixteen regions listed above are generally considered to be the most promising regions in the six counties although there are at least half a dozen other areas, the most prominent of which is Keller and vicinity in Ferry County, which should be considered.

One of the most important tools of the researcher is an original map. Old maps may sometimes be found in the larger libraries, local or county museums and usually in state and university archives.

At the discretion of the librarian, curator or director, certain individuals may be given permission to examine and perhaps purchase a photo-copy from the institution. Serious researchers are cautioned to procure historic (copy) maps and current maps before embarking on an expedition into an unfamiliar area. Other publications are available from various state agencies such as the Department of Natural Resources, Division of Geology and Earth Resources. Many other books, from both governmental agencies and private presses have information which may assist greatly in pinpointing areas of special interest.

Once a certain area or ghost town site has been decided upon, it is wise to study an original copy map and any historic photographs or prints available. By using all of these archival aids, a much clearer picture of the original town begins to emerge. Fire insurance maps and plans invariably indicate where boardwalks ran, where doors and other entrances to buildings were located. If you are using an insurance map look for hotels and the saloon door, I have recovered up to 72 coins, some of them lying visible on the surface, in front of a saloon door. Another important feature are the boardwalks. Most of the old wooden boardwalks have long rotted away but the ground that was beneath them is still intact, and often the coins which slipped through the cracks and knotholes in the original boardwalk are still lying exactly where they were lost those many decades ago. If you are short of time, it is a good idea to determine the width of the boards and then sweep both the outside and inside edges of the walk with your detector. If you're using a screen instead of a detector, screen the dirt down until you come to a relatively "clean" layer of dirt. When you reach this clean layer it almost always means that the coins are above this layer. The presence of marbles, nails and especially buttons are invariably good

Some of almost $47,000 worth of raw silver found by the author. Most of the silver ore was converted into silver bars like those shown.

indicators that coins lie close at hand.

Strangely, most of the coins recovered from boardwalk areas are silver, generally there are few nickels or coppers - and only rarely gold pieces. The majority of the coins are located near the entrances to old saloon, hotel, general store and bank sites, with considerably smaller concentrations in front of other less used establishments.

The advantage in using a screen instead of a detector is that a screen never misses whereas a detector, even in the hands of a skilled operator, can and surprisingly often, does miss. The disadvantage of a screen is that it is extremely slow work, and it is laborious work. To elaborate on this statement, in the summer of 1985 I was re-working a section of boardwalk in an historic silver mining town, the section was 8' wide by 24' long and had been swept by at least three or four dozen coin shooters. In one and one-half days of screening I recovered 63 coins and 1 poker chip, 54 of the coins were silver, including two half dollars. Most of the coins pre-dated 1920 and the oldest was an 1872 quarter - and the metal detectors had missed all of these coins!

Most successful treasure hunters use both a metal detector and a screen, the detector for the initial sweep and to find hot spots, and then the screen to check.

Three gold coins, two in excellent condition, found in the drawer of an old desk. Caches of valuable coins were hidden in a wide variety of unusual hiding places. The condition of the coins is of paramount importance.

COLLECTABLES

Part of the author's large collection of Chinese artifacts. Most of the items pictured were recovered from an old Chinese store. The three old porcelain figures shown are the so-called "Three Kings." Also pictured are gold and silver jewellery items and various other pieces found in the store and in trunks on the premises.

The categories which are listed below include the majority of the fields of collecting in general Western Americana. In this chapter some of the particulars of these items are elaborated upon. This section is included merely as a guide for the average collector.

1. Banknotes
2. Bird's Eye View Maps
3. Books
4. Bottles
5. Checks
6. Chinese Items
7. Coins
8. Firearms
9. Gambling Memorabilia
10. General Store Items
11. Gold Scales and Mining Equipment
12. Hotel Items
13. Indian Artifacts
14. Lawmen's Equipment
15. Letters, Diaries, Newspapers and ephemera
16. Maps
17. Paintings
18. Photographs
19. Postcards
20. Railroad Memorabilia
21. Ranching Equipment
22. Saloon Items
23. Siphons
24. Stock Certificates
25. Strongboxes and safes
26. Tins
27. Tokens
28. Toys
29. Wells, Fargo & Company items
30. General and Miscellaneous

In nearly every instance the condition, rarity, collectability and history of an item affect its historical and its monetary value. Diaries, letters and other important records are usually considered of archival value and should be housed in a suitable institution; generally a local or county museum or a university archives. If at all possible, these items should be retained in the area of origin.

BANKNOTES ● Early fractional notes, federal government and privately issued banknotes are all collector's items. The condition of any old banknotes is important as is the rarity, color, signatures, date of issue and denomination. Specimens are often found in coin collections or occasionally in caches or other unusual hiding places.

Some fractional notes and private bank issues are pictured along with a rare two ounce Wells, Fargo & Company silver bar. All of the items shown above range in value from $10 to $150.

BIRD'S EYE VIEW MAPS ● These large maps, generally published from the 1880s to the turn of the century, depict a specific city; streets and avenues, businesses, houses, rivers and other features in great detail. Usually printed on linen and generally in black and white, the prices vary from around $100 to $1,000 and occasionally more. Condition and rarity are the two most important factors affecting price. These maps are usually found in larger cities like Spokane and Seattle.

BOOKS ● Books about Washington, especially if the work was published prior to 1915 and contains maps, illustrations, photographs, colored plates or prints, are collectable. Condition is extremely important, as is rarity, author, edition and subject. Subjects such as Indians, county histories, general histories, railroads, militaria, ranching, birds, mammals, mining and other similar categories are collectable. Certain older atlases, especially with maps of the west, are usually worth examining. Original wraps and dust jackets should be kept. The prices of old books vary widely, from about 25¢ to $500.00 or perhaps more for a very rare book in exceptionally fine condition. Generally, rare books are found in private collections or in estate sales.

Great Northern lamp and railroader's cap and kerchief. In the past decade collectors have concentrated on railroad memorabilia. It is becoming increasingly difficult to obtain the harder to get items, especially from the defunct lines.

BOTTLES ● This is a popular category and the majority of collectors have bottles in their collections. The rarest bottles are generally found in or around the oldest towns or in the dumps of ghost towns or old mining camps. Nearly all embossed bottles are worth collecting. Rarity, type of mould, embossing, age, shape, color and of course, condition, are all important factors in establishing the worth of a bottle. Original labels also enhance the value considerably. At the height of the bottle craze during the 1960s, most of the dumps in the state were combed, although, surprisingly, new finds continue to turn up in the old areas, but usually in more isolated locations and the dumps are often overgrown, much deeper and more difficult to locate. Most embossed whiskies, beers and wines command reasonably high prices even today, although the prices are lower than in the heyday. Pottery items are increasingly in demand, especially those marked with company names.

CHECKS ● Increasing in popularity. Old bank checks, especially those from now defunct banks, are sought after. Prices are usually around a low of 25¢ to highs of $10.00, although rarer ghost town bank checks, from places like Molson, sometimes run higher. Checks from old banks in places like Roslyn, Republic, Northport and other historic mining towns are generally more desirable. Attractiveness, condition, color, date and signature are all important.

CHINESE ITEMS ● More or less neglected for years, except by a small and enthusiastic group of collectors, Chinese artifacts have suddenly come into their own. There are literally hundreds of items which fall under this category. Medicine bottles, beers, brass opium tins, brass holed coins and a variety of earthenware pots and jugs are relatively common, even today. Other artifacts falling under the rare label would include gold and opium scales, porcelain figures, tools, signs, games of chance, placer mining items, articles of clothing, hats, decorated bowls, musical instruments, jewellery, jade and a truly wide variety of other lesser known articles. Prices range from lows of about $1.50 for common medicine bottles through to middle range items like cased gold scales which usually run from $70.00 to $100.00 and up into the much rarer items of porcelain, jewellery and jade. Some of the latter command extremely high prices, sometimes well into the hundreds and in certain instances into the thousand dollar plus range. This is in the realm of the expert and anyone unsure of the worth of a specific item should contact a reputable expert on Chinese antiques. Anywhere where there was a large Chinese community or camp is worth browsing around. Any written records are considered in the public domain and should be made available to public institutions. Chinese items should be, if at all possible, well documented, otherwise their value will be adversely affected.

COINS ● Another specialized field. Numismatics is one of the most exacting of hobbies and one of the most interesting. The collectors fall into numerous categories; some collect only gold coins, or silver dollars or dimes or some other specific type of coin. Others collect almost every type of coin. It can be an expensive and time consuming pastime but there are certain criteria which every collector should be aware of. Condition is of paramount importance and so is rarity. If a specific coin is rare and is in mint condition, it will often sell for many times that of a duplicate coin in poor condition. Collectors are cautioned not to clean coins, leave that to the experts. Any privately struck gold coins from California, Utah, Colorado, Oregon or Georgia are highly prized, with certain rare coins like the J. S. Ormsby $10 gold piece valued at well over $100,000.00, or the Cincinatti Mining

& Trading Co. 1849 $10 gold piece probably worth $300,000.00 or more. R. S. Yeoman's "Guide Book of United States Coins" is considered the most comprehensive guide to prices.

FIREARMS ● Certainly a category which has been a collector's favorite for generations. Colt, Winchester, Remington and scores of other arms manufacturers have produced thousands of guns. Again rarity and condition are of paramount importance. Collectors are advised to deal with well established gun dealers. Prices vary widely, from as low as $10.00 for a common gun in poor condition to many thousands for a gun of unusual rarity and condition.

GAMBLING MEMORABILIA ● Many fascinating items belong in this field of collecting. Old games of chance like roulette wheels or wheels of fortune are becoming rare and may run anywhere from $1,000.00 or well over that sum if they are in good condition and are well documented. Other gambling items like monogrammed poker chips or the rarer ivory chips are attractive and collectable. Old decks of playing cards, old dice, dice cups and cages, brass slot machines, hold-out devices, faro layouts, dealing boxes, casekeepers and any other paraphernalia which was associated with the early gambling fraternity.

GENERAL STORE ITEMS ● A wide array of equipment and items are found in this category; large wheeled coffee mills, various types of scales, nickel-plated or brass cash registers, fixtures, candy jars and other containers, lamps, tobacco cutters and cheese slicers are only a few

Rare ivory poker chips - circa 1890

of the scores of items in this collecting field. Prices vary from the large wheeled coffee mill at $750.00 and upwards to as little as $5.00 for a mediocre candy jar.

<u>GOLD SCALES AND MINING EQUIPMENT</u> ● This category is indelibly linked with the early history of the West. It is becoming increasingly difficult to obtain some of the scarcer items in this field. Original gold scales with troy weights, especially the boxed and stand-up sets are now hard to find and range anywhere from a low of $75.00 to well over $1,000.00 for an ornate and historical set. Leather gold pokes, early type gold pans, original rockers, old miner's picks, riveted shovels, mercury flasks, old copper blowing pans, sniping tools and many other items relating to placer mining are being avidly collected. Hard-rock mining equipment including mortars and pestles, ore cars, old carbide lamps, dynamite boxes, blasting cap tins, carbide tins, miner's lamps and assay scales are just a few of the many hard-rock collectables. A collector should be aware that condition, rarity, specific history and general attractiveness are all important factors in determining value.

An unusually fine set of Chinese gold scales - circa 1860. This set was found in an abandoned shed in an old placer gold camp in 1948. It was covered with six inches of ice, and the unusual brass Chinese weights were found close by. There was also an old Wells, Fargo & Co. safe in the back of the shed. The figure eight weights are seldom seen today.

HOTEL ITEMS ● Also being collected increasingly. Some of the items are pitcher and basin sets, cash registers, monogrammed hotel plates, menu cards, brass key returns, hotel registers and a handful of other articles which were found in the early hotels.

INDIAN ARTIFACTS ● There is an ongoing controversy about the ethics of collecting certain Indian artifacts. There is, however, an active and long established trade in beads, weaponry, coiled baskets, tools, decorative leatherwork and chipped implements. It is now considered to be unethical and indeed unlawful to excavate prehistoric burial sites or other important sites which indeed lie within the province of the professional archaeologist. It is extremely important, however, for a collector to carefully document and catalogue every artifact and item in his collection, otherwise they will have little historic value.

LAWMEN'S EQUIPMENT ● A handful of dedicated collectors have quietly and steadily been collecting these items for years, and only recently have the general public been aware of the historic significance of the early lawman's equipment. Original badges; beware of numerous spurious specimens, gunbelts, sawed-off shotguns, revolvers, 'wanted' circulars or posters, handcuffs, legirons and other early equipment used by the old time lawman are becoming extremely hard to find. The prices range from as low as $25.00 for an undocumented pair of handcuffs, to well over $1,000.00 for a revolver once owned by a well known lawman. This

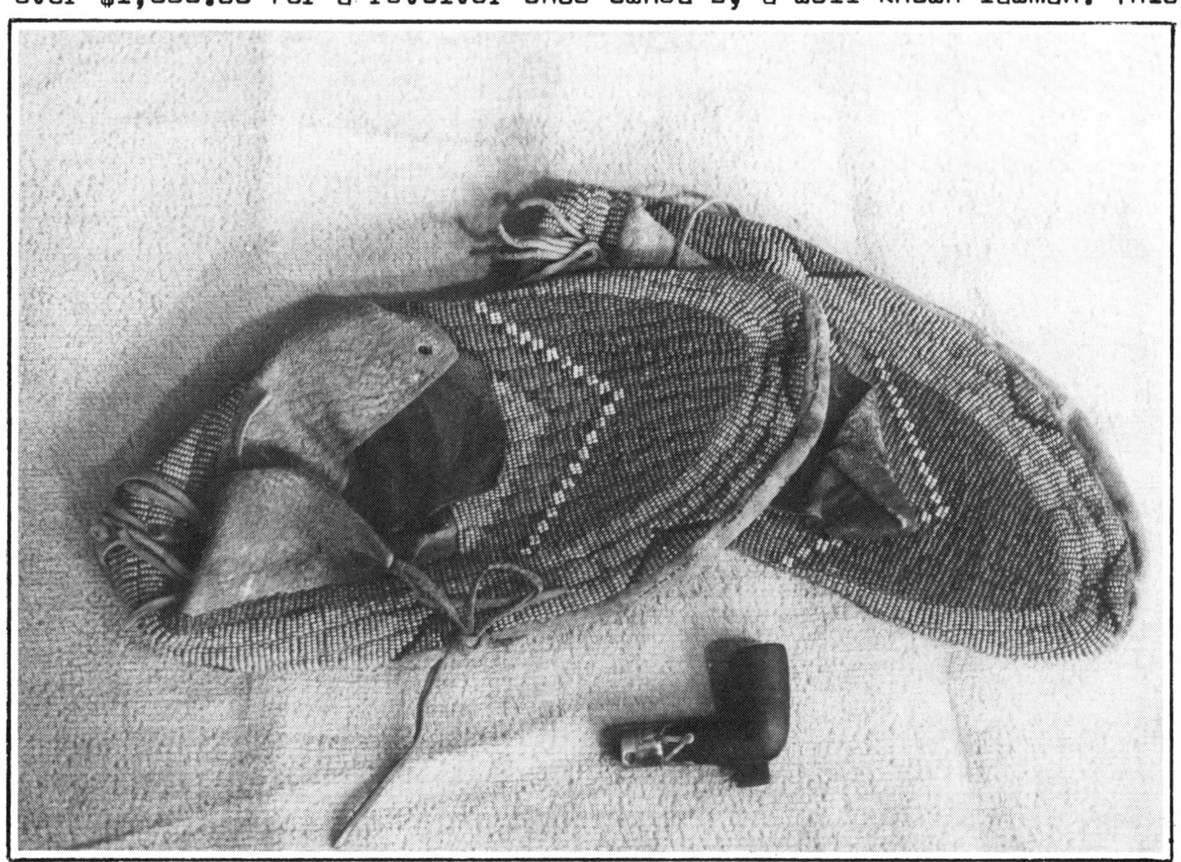

Fully beaded Blackfoot moccasins and trade pipe without stem.

particular field, however, has attracted some unscrupulous individuals and dealers. Although they are a distinct minority, both sellers and purchasers should exercise caution before buying or selling.

LETTERS, DIARIES, NEWSPAPERS and EPHEMERA ● This category has long been considered within the realm of county, university, state or other public institutions or archives. It is generally considered unethical to sell an item that should be housed in a public archives. There is, however, an active trade in lesser items which fall under this particular category. Old newspapers (pre 1915), broadsides, letters with original covers (envelopes), notices, advertisements, receipts, paper tickets, circus flyers and scores of other paper items all belong in this field. Prices vary considerably from as low as $1.00 for a common newspaper (circa 1930), to many thousands of dollars for an unusually rare "express" cover or envelope. Historical importance, date, rarity, condition, general attractiveness, authenticity and documentation all enhance value. Condition, of course, is of primary importance.

MAPS ● A widely collected item which is gaining in popularity. This is also a field which interests archivists as well as collectors. The most important maps usually pre-date 1900 and were drawn by well-known

A very rare Winchester & Main saddle holster with a lawman's 1875 Colt and original holster and a gun belt.

cartographers, although there were some exceptions. Early exploration, mining, railroad, townsite and numerous other types of maps are being avidly collected by those interested in Western Americana. Rarity and condition are extremely important factors in determining the value of a map. Other considerations would include color, date, scale, general collectability and artistic embellishments. Prices range from lows of $1.00 to $5.00 to thousands of dollars for a particularly rare map in excellent condition. Even old hand-drawn maps are often valuable - if they are signed, dated and authenticed.

PAINTINGS ● A specialist's field and not for the uninitiated. It is extremely unlikely that anyone has an unknown painting by artists like Remington, Russell, Catlin, Bodmer, Kane or Tavernier or any others in the first rank of western painters. It would also be equally unlikely that uncatalogued paintings by artists like A. J. Miller, W. R. Leigh, A. Bierstadt, Henry F. Farny, John Mix Stanley, Peter Rindisbacher or O. C. Seltzer are lying around. However, other works by lesser Western artists have turned up from time to time and many of these paintings, or sketches, are very valuable and often bring sums of a few hundred dollars to many thousands. A major work by Russell or Remington might well run into well over $100,000.00. Beware of fakes which are always around. Most paintings have signatures and are dated, although there

C. M. Russell's 1902 oil entitled "When Sioux and Blackfeet Meet." A fine Russell or Remington usually runs into hundreds of thousands of dollars in the Western art market.

are exceptions to this rule. Anyone possessing an old painting which they suspect might be valuable would be wise to have it examined by a reputable art dealer or art auctioneer.

PHOTOGRAPHS ● An important field which has gained many adherents in the past decade or so. Old, original photographs if they are in good condition and not faded usually range from a low of $5.00 to a high of around $50.00 unless it is of exceptional historic significance. If it happens to portray a hanging, a fire, an outlaw, an accident or some other significant event it may be quite valuable. Carpenter, Matsura, Hegg, Trueman or some other well known old-time photographers will be considerably more valuable than an unknown amateur generally. Indians or Indian scenes, placer mining scenes, stagecoaches, trains, saloons or hotels, street scenes, ghost towns, sternwheelers, hardrock mines, sporting events, lawmen or outlaws, famous or infamous individuals or some other scene of historic interest add to the value. Family photos are commonplace and are generally valueless except to the family for sentimental reasons. Albums by well known photographers with original photographs dating 1900 or before are usually valuable.

POSTCARDS ● Still well within the reach of the average collector or Old West enthusiast. Postcards are available in most antique shops or at swap meets. Prices usually run anywhere from as low as 25¢ for an

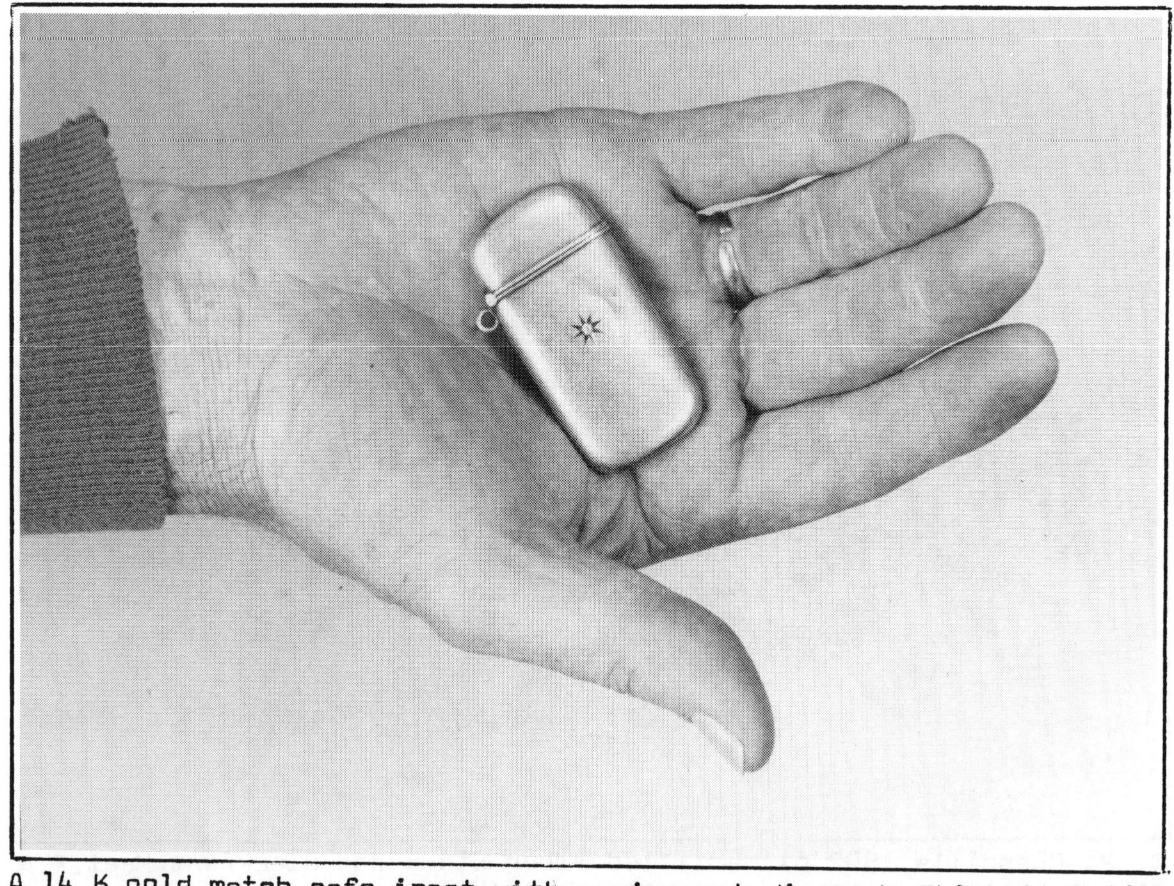

A 14 K gold match safe inset with a mine cut diamond. This attractive item was once owned by a lady of leisure.

unimpressive postcard to around $15.00, and occasionally more, for a particularly fine card which portrays a classic scene; a ghost town, Indians, placer miners, stagecoaches, trains or some other historic, and unusual, scene. Generally black and white postcards have a sharp image whereas color cards are more attractive. Both photographs and postcards should be stored in acid free envelopes.

RAILROAD MEMORABILIA ● This colorful part of the early history of the state has long attracted a cross section of collectors. A number of railroads provided early transportation into the interior of the state, notably James J. Hill's Great Northern. All memorabilia from these pioneer lines are collectable. Some of the items to watch for are; signs, tools, uniforms. caps, hats, badges, strongboxes, locks, keys, lanterns, maps, tickets and other paper items. Almost any item identified with an early railroad is worth keeping. A good, original sign may bring $500.00 or more, a strongbox in fine condition may be worth in the neighborhood of $300.00 or more. Beware of reproduction signs. It is generally agreed that this category will appreciate in value quite rapidly in the next few years.

An unusually fine Great Northern Railway sign and strongbox from the Nighthawk region. Courtesy Bud and Lucy Shull Collection, Brewster.

RANCHING EQUIPMENT ● Another field of collecting where items are becoming much higher priced and increasingly hard to obtain. In this attractive category there are a number of pieces: saddles, bridles, bits, working spurs, show spurs, branding irons (including "running irons"), saddle bags, hats, belts, lariats, barbed wire (especially early types), shotgun, stovepipe and wooly chaps, old brand books, signs and any other items associated with the frontier ranching era. Rare saddles sometimes bring over $1,000.00 and an especially fine pair of documented "wooly" chaps often runs $500.00 or more. If the history of the article is included, this usually enhances the value of the piece.

SALOON ITEMS ● A restricted number of items in this category, and they are becoming rarer. Brass spitoons (watch for fakes), bar-room paintings, the most famous of which are the various battle scenes of "Custer's Last Stand", etched advertising mirrors, chandeliers, poker or other games tables, saloon cash registers and other paraphernalia from the early saloons.

SIPHONS ● Becoming more popular with collectors, especially when the company and town names are embossed on them. Colored siphons are usually more valuable. Prices vary from $20.00 to well over $150.00 and occasionally more for an exceptionally rare piece.

Cuffs decorated with coin silver and brass, silver spurs and barbed wire stretcher are just a few of the ranching collectables.

STOCK CERTIFICATES ● Generally an inexpensive and attractive item for collectors of Western Americana. Stock certificates dated prior to 1900 are usually more valuable. Color, art work, rarity, name of the company (mining and railroads are popular), signatures and even the number of shares issued all have a bearing on the value. Almost all stock certificates are located in estates or lawyer's offices. Common, recent stock certificates sometimes fetch only 25¢ or even less, whereas rare and unusually picturesque stock certificates may bring up to $50.00. Condition, as usual, is important.

STRONGBOXES and SAFES ● Once a glut on the market, both of these items are very difficult to find now. Good strongboxes run anywhere from $100.00 to $500.00 and occasionally more. A finely painted safe may be obtained for as little as $50.00 but it may bring as much as $800.00 if it has the original company name on it and originated in a famous mining town or ghost town and was once owned by a citizen of some notoriety.

TINS ● Once commonplace, fine tins have increased dramatically in price in the past eight years. Some tins may be in the $5.00 range, others, extremely rare and in fine condition, have sold for as much as $1,200.00. Tobacco tins, coffee tins, tea tins and nearly every

A gold scales with a set of brass troy weights. This set, like many others, was manufactured in Philadelphia.

other type of tin imaginable has a market. Condition is probably the most important factor affecting price, with decorative embellishment and rarity close behind. Pictorial scenes are generally popular. The number of tins turning up remains fairly steady although the supply of good tins is drying up.

TOKENS ● By the 1890s, many merchants were issuing tokens. Designed to encourage repeat business, tokens came in a variety of shapes and metals. The early pieces were usually made of brass, aluminum, German silver or copper. Most tokens issued prior to 1930 have some value, sometimes low, occasionally surprisingly high. Tokens from old ghost towns and mining towns like Loomis, Conconully, Republic, Winthrop, Nelson (now Danville), Chesaw and a few other places are quite rare and usually bring anywhere from $40.00 to as much as $100.00 for an unusually fine one-of-a-kind token. Places like Northport, Metaline Falls, Molson and Curlew are a little easier to obtain and generally run from $5.00 to $20.00. More common pieces from towns like Chelan, Omak, Roslyn, Brewster, Wenatchee, Peshastin and many other towns in the interior may be purchased for as low as $1.00 each, depending on the number available. Condition is important but so is rarity. A one-of-a-kind token from Loomis is a real find whereas a hundred of the same kind would bring a very low price.

Tokens from various towns in the six counties. Hundreds of merchants issued tokens, especially from 1890 to 1915. Prices generally depend upon rarity and condition. Several rare pieces are pictured above.

TOYS ● All types of toys, usually pre-dating 1950, are being picked up by discerning collectors. This field is almost never ending as the choice runs from pull toys to wind-ups, from lead soldiers to painted toy boxes, from dolls to teddy bears. The prices vary widely, from a few dollars to thousands of dollars. Condition is all important as is rarity and uniqueness. Toys should not be repainted and all original boxes should be retained as they enhance the value. Beware of fakes, especially in cast toys like banks.

WELLS, FARGO & COMPANY ITEMS ● Shotguns, strongboxes, signs, locks, badges, franked covers (envelopes), caps, badges and almost all items from this most renowned express and banking company are being sought by intelligent collectors. Nearly all Wells, Fargo articles have been marked "W. F. & Co." or "Wells, Fargo & Co." These are among the most coveted of all Western Americana collectables.

OTHER AND MISCELLANEOUS ● The list is practically endless. Buttons, jewellery, insulators, glassware, prints, tools, advertising, badges, flags, militaria, mineral specimens, clothes (certain periods), keys, locks, quilts, stained glass and so on. Collectors should be careful when purchasing an item and are advised to avoid buying antiques in a field they are not familiar with. Sellers would be wise to get several expert opinions before parting with an item of unknown value.

Wells, Fargo & Co. sawed-off shotgun. Marked W. F. & Co. No. 842, it was used by company guards. In front is a Wells, Fargo wagon sign.

Other Great Hancock House Titles

Guide to Gold Panning
N. L. Barlee
ISBN 0-88839-986-3
8½ x 11, SC, 192 pp.

Gold Creeks & Ghost Towns (BC)
N. L. Barlee
ISBN 0-88839-988-X
8½ x 11, SC, 192 pp.

Lost Mines & Historic Treasures
N. L. Barlee
ISBN 0-88839-992-8
8½ x 11, SC, 96 pp.

Guide to Similkameen Treasure
N. L. Barlee
ISBN 0-88839-990-1
8½ x 11, SC, 96 pp.

Great Western Train Robberies
Don DeNevi
ISBN 0-88839-287-7
5½ x 8½, 202 pp

Gold! Gold!
Joseph F. Petralia
ISBN 0-88839-118-8
5½ x 8½, 110 pp

Buckskins, Blades and Biscuits
Allen Johnston
ISBN 0-88839-363-6
5½ x 8½, 176 pp

Guide for Weekend Prospectors
S. F. Wayland
ISBN 0-88839-405-5
5½ x 8½, 96 pp